BY KENNETH BUDD

Be Reasonable!

How Community Associations Can Enforce
Rules Without Antagonizing Residents,
Going to Court, or Starting World War III

community
ASSOCIATIONS INSTITUTE

225 Reinekers Lane, Suite 300 ∎ Alexandria, Virginia 22314 ∎ 703/548-8600
Fax 703/684-1581 ∎ www.caionline.org

COMMUNITY ASSOCIATIONS INSTITUTE
225 REINEKERS LANE, SUITE 300
ALEXANDRIA, VA 22314

The Community Associations Institute is a national, nonprofit association created in 1973 to educate and represent America's residential community association industry. It is a multidisciplinary alliance leading the industry and fostering effective community associations.

Library of Congress Cataloging-in-Publication Data

Budd, Kenneth M., 1966– .
Be Reasonable!: How Community Associations Can Enforce Rules Without Antagonizing
    Residents, Going to Court, or Starting World War III / by Kenneth Budd.
        p. cm.
    Includes bibliographical references and index.
    ISBN 0-941301-40-0
        1. Real covenants—United States—Popular works. 2. Homeowners' associations—
    Law and legislation—United States—Popular works.
I. Community Associations Institute. II. Title.
KF662.Z9B83   1998
346.7304'32—DC21   97-48826
                                                                        CIP

Cover illustration/design by Cori Froelich Canady

ACKNOWLEDGMENTS

The author and the Community Associations Institute would like to thank the many volunteers who have written articles for *Common Ground* magazine or contributed their expertise as sources. Much of their advice is found in this book. CAI also thanks the following individuals who donated their time and energy to review *Be Reasonable!*:

Ralph C. Baxter and **James Henry**
George Mason University
Fairfax, Virginia

Samuel L. Dolnick
La Mesa, California

Ross W. Feinberg
Feldsott, Lee & Feinberg
Newport Beach, California

Thomas J. Hindman
Orten & Hindman, P.C.
Denver, Colorado

Stephen M. Marcus
Marcus, Goodman, Emmer & Brooks, P.C.
Braintree, Massachusetts

Marvin J. Nodiff
Nodiff & Ellis, Attorneys at Law
St. Louis, Missouri

Vivian G. Walker, Ph.D.
Felix Staff/Service Development Institute
Honolulu, Hawaii

CONTENTS

INTRODUCTION

"We've spent years hammering
directors on how they could be held
personally liable if they failed to
enforce the CC&Rs. We neglected
to teach them about reasonableness
and flexibility."

—*Brent Herrington, PCAM,*
community manager in Florida

On a June day in 1991, Helen Garrett spotted
a notice above the mailboxes at her Santa
Ana, California condominium. The notice accused Garrett, a 51-year-old financial consultant and
grandmother, of "parking in [a] circular driveway...kissing
and doing bad things for over one hour." Her condominium association, which posted the notice, promised to
fine her if it caught her doing "bad things" in the future.

Garrett was furious. Her kiss with "a very respected
businessman" was brief. People began calling her "hot
lips," she said, and asked her what bad things she was doing. The story quickly became national news, appearing in
the *Los Angeles Times* and *USA Today*. Garrett hired a high-

profile attorney. She threatened to sue for defamation and emotional distress, and demanded a public apology. She received it only when the association learned the "violator" was not Garrett but a 17-year-old girl and her boyfriend.[1]

This is a textbook example of an unreasonable board of directors. The association board never passed a rule against "kissing and doing bad things;" it never had the authority to peek into residents' cars. And even if such a rule existed, it's so unreasonable—a kiss goodnight is hardly the association's business, let alone a threat to property values—that no court would support it.

The board's enforcement procedures were equally unreasonable. Rather than notifying Garrett of the violation in private, or issuing a warning, or offering due process, the association chose public humiliation, posting the violation notice where anyone could see it. And how did it intend to enforce the rule? Would the condo kiss police fine her $50 for every smooch? Would they run lipstick tests on every man who exited the community? And what, exactly, is the legal definition of "bad thing?"

In this case, the "bad thing" was a bad rule—and equally bad enforcement procedures.

Harassing residents is not why community associations have rules and restrictions. Community associations enforce rules and restrictions to ensure a high quality of life for residents and to preserve property values. To prevent homeowners from painting their houses pink or storing washing machines in their yards. The problem is that many directors—as in the case of Helen Garrett—are overzealous. Or inflexible. They overstep their legal bounds of authority. They write rules that are vague and imprecise; that are too broad and too extreme. Rules that serve no purpose in maintaining property values. Rules that are outdated, illogical, and unreasonable.

Enforcing rules and restrictions doesn't need to result in unnecessary lawsuits and public relations nightmares. This book offers strategies for drafting and enacting reasonable rules, identifying unreasonable rules and restrictions, and working with owners. It also discusses reasonable enforcement procedures, from making exceptions to providing due process.

Much of this information is based on articles I've written for *Common Ground*—a bimonthly magazine on condominium and homeowner associations published by the Community Associations Institute (CAI). Since 1990, I've written over 50 feature articles on community associations, most of them on the need to be reasonable. Here, then, is how your community association can enforce rules and restrictions without antagonizing neighbors, going to court, or starting World War III.

CHAPTER ONE

Writing Reasonable Rules

"If a rule is reasonable, the
association can adopt it;
if not, it cannot."

—*Ruling from the 1975 case*
Hidden Harbor Estates, Inc. *v.* Norman

"A man's home is his castle." These are sacred words
for many Americans. But in a common-interest
community, a man's home *isn't* his castle.
Homeowners can't do whatever they want. They can't
paint their houses pink. Often they can't place political
signs in their yard or they can't park trucks in the community lot.

That's the nature of common-interest living. When
you buy a home in a common-interest community, be it a
condominium unit, townhome, or single-family home, you
agree to abide by rules and restrictions. You live close to
your neighbors, you share common facilities, and you sac-
rifice certain freedoms—voluntarily—to protect property
values and reduce nuisances.

Many homeowners don't know this. They move into
a common-interest community without reviewing the re-

strictions and are shocked to learn—after receiving a stern letter from
their community association—that their choice of house paints violates the covenants. Or that their beloved family dog is too big. Or
that they can't run their business from their home.

Rules and restrictions can seem petty and invasive to new residents (or to residents who violate them). But they serve a purpose.
They prevent nuisance problems and preserve aesthetic harmony.
They prevent owners from blasting their stereos at 4:00 a.m.; from
breeding boa constrictors on their balconies; or from turning their
yards into car lots. Reasonable restrictions, consistently enforced
over time, preserve property values and maintain a high quality of life
for residents.

Understanding Rules and Restrictions

The goals of rules and restrictions are to:

■ Preserve, protect, and enhance a community's property values and
   assets
■ Promote harmonious living
■ Ensure that residents can use and enjoy the property

Community association restrictions consist primarily of covenants and rules. **Covenants** are restrictions written by the
community's developer and included in the community's governing
documents. A board of directors inherits the enforcement of covenants when it assumes control of the association. In condominiums,
the covenants (also known as "deed restrictions") are found in the
Declaration or Master Deed; in cooperatives they're in the Proprietary Lease. Covenants for planned communities are included in the
Declaration of Covenants, Conditions, and Restrictions (CC&Rs).

Covenants typically affect the fundamental use of the property.
They usually can be changed only by amending the governing documents. Most documents require a large percentage of owners and
mortgagees to vote in favor of an amendment (see pages 69–71).

Rules are generally written by the board of directors. Board
members adopt rules and regulations through policy resolutions; in
some cases they are adopted by a vote of the members. A policy

resolution deals with the use of common areas and recreational facilities, architectural guidelines, and enforcement procedures. It is a motion that affects the owners' rights and obligations. If the board wants to pass a rule requiring owners to clean up after their pets, for example, it would do so by introducing a policy resolution at a board meeting. Or, it could simply approve a motion amending existing rules.

Rules and covenants must comply with state and local laws. CAI's M-100 course[1] ranks the hierarchy of authority as follows:

- Federal law, regulations, and court decisions
- State law, regulations, and court decisions
- City and county law, regulations, and court decisions
- Declaration, CC&R, master deed, proprietary lease, or occupancy agreement
- Articles of Incorporation
- Bylaws
- Board resolutions

Rules should not conflict with these higher forms of authority. Otherwise, they may be unenforceable.

(For this book, restrictions based in the association's governing documents, such as covenants, will be called "restrictions." Those created by the board will be called "rules and regulations.")

What Is Reasonable?

A reasonable rule or restriction is logical. It addresses a specific problem with a specific solution that is rational and fair. It is neither too broad nor too restrictive.

Common sense is usually the best judge. It's reasonable, for example, to restrict dogs from destroying property or running without a leash. It's not reasonable to ban pets from common areas—a rule that has forced some owners to wheel their pets in baby carriages when taking them outside. A Massachusetts condominium association prohibited pets from leaving their units entirely. For pet owners Rhonda and William Dean, this meant sneaking their 70-pound dog to the car—without letting his paws touch the ground, of course— then driving him outside the community to relieve himself. Two years later, a judge declared that the rule was unreasonable.[2]

Likewise, consider an association where teenagers ride skateboards late into the night, disturbing neighbors while they're trying to sleep. The problem isn't the kids or the skateboards, but *when* the kids are skating. A reasonable rule would prohibit skateboarding during nighttime hours—for example, from 10:00 p.m. to 8:00 a.m. An unreasonable rule would ban skateboards and forbid children from playing outside.

Sample Cases

"It is sometimes difficult to determine whether a court will consider a particular rule reasonable," writes former CAI President Katharine Rosenberry. "For example, some courts have concluded that prohibiting recreational vehicles in a condominium community is reasonable and others have concluded that it is not. Courts generally agree, however, that rules that only apply to one or a few owners, or that are unfair to a segment of owners, cannot be enforced. While most courts give the board some latitude in rules enforcement, courts are more likely to enforce rules that are reasonable and that treat owners fairly."[3]

Several courts have tried to define "reasonable." In *Hidden Harbor Estates, Inc. v. Norman*,[4] a landmark 1975 case, a Florida condo owner challenged an association rule against alcohol consumption in common areas. The court found that the rule was reasonable and established a "reasonableness" test:

> Certainly, the association is not at liberty to adopt arbitrary or capricious rules bearing no relationship to the health, happiness and enjoyment of life of the various unit owners. On the contrary, we believe the test is reasonableness. If a rule is reasonable, the association can adopt it; if not, it cannot.[5]

The *Norman* case would resurface in a significant 1994 case: *Nahrstedt v. Lakeside Village Condominium Association, Inc.*[6] Natore Nahrstedt sued the Lakeside Village association after it fined her for keeping three cats—Boo Boo, Tulip, and Dockers—in violation of its ban against pets (which was contained in the recorded documents). Nahrstedt asked the court to repeal the pet restriction and the fines, and claimed emotional distress and invasion of privacy. The California Supreme Court ruled that the no-pet restriction was reasonable for the community as a whole.

The court stated that association restrictions are generally enforceable unless they:

■ Violate a fundamental public policy
■ Bear no rational relationship to the protection, preservation, operation, or purpose of the affected land
■ Create more harmful effects on homeowners' land use than benefits

"In determining whether a restriction is 'unreasonable,'" wrote the court, "the focus is on the restriction's effect on the project as a whole, not on the individual homeowner."[7] This was a new standard for the rule of reasonableness. The court ruled that restrictions should be enforced "unless they are wholly arbitrary, violate a fundamental public policy, or impose a burden on the use of affected land that far outweighs any benefit."[8]

The *Nahrstedt* test played a large role in the 1995 case *Liebler* v. *Point Loma Tennis Club*. In 1992, the board learned that Liebler—a nonresident owner—was using the California community's tennis courts. This violated its rules, which prohibit nonresident owners from using the facilities. The association began fining Liebler when he refused to turn in his recreation card. Liebler filed suit, arguing that the association lacked the authority to enact the rule or to impose fines. Using the *Nahrstedt* decision, an appeals court upheld the association rule. The rule, it said, was valid and reasonable because it was not arbitrary. "There are valid reasons why members of a tennis-oriented residential condominium might choose to restrict access to their private tennis courts," wrote the court, "since maintaining a low density ensures the courts will be available to residents, families and guests."[9]

Wayne S. Hyatt and Jo Anne P. Stubblefield note that decisions in the California case *Laguna Royale Owners Association* v. *Darger*[10] and the Florida case *Beachwood Villas Condominium* v. *Poor*[11] offer common approaches toward applying the rule of reasonableness. Associations must act in a fair and nondiscriminatory manner in exercising their powers. They must make decisions that are rationally related to the protection, preservation, and proper operation of the property and the association's purpose as defined in the governing documents.[12]

These cases are simply examples of how some courts interpret reasonability. The attorneys who reviewed *Be Reasonable!* note that reasonableness can be interpreted quite differently from state to state. Still, certain assumptions can be made. Restrictions based in the declaration are generally given a "a strong presumption of validity"[13] since owners agree to abide by them when they buy their home. Rules adopted by the board are more likely to be scrutinized by courts. Rational rules and restrictions that are rationally enforced—and that promote a legitimate goal—will generally be considered reasonable. And remember: even reasonable rules should not be enforced in unreasonable circumstances (see pages 38–40).

In all of these cases, the message of the *Norman* decision still holds true: "If a rule is reasonable the association can adopt it; if not, it cannot."

What Is Unreasonable?

If reasonable rules and restrictions promote legitimate goals, unreasonable rules and restrictions promote illegitimate goals. They are illogical or unfair; too broad or too severe.

According to M. Edward Burns, a Colorado attorney and the author of CAI's *Pet Peeves*, unreasonable rules and restrictions usually result from snap decisions that don't address the real problem. Restricting dogs based on their size, for example, doesn't solve the problems normally associated with pets: loud barking and owners who neglect to clean pet waste.

"The biggest problems occur when boards make knee-jerk rules," said Burns. "If boards would sit down and articulate the problem, and find a reasonable way to address it, the resulting rule is usually upheld by [the] courts."[14]

To determine if a rule or restriction is unreasonable, take the following test:

1. Is it based on outdated notions? Many community association documents were written 20 to 30 years ago. As a result, they
contain outdated covenants. Bans against trucks made sense 30 years
ago. Trucks were TRUCKS—muddy monstrosities for carrying tim-
ber. Satellite dishes were six-feet wide. Home businesses were
banned because they meant traffic and noise—no one imagined personal computers, modems, and home offices.

"Older documents have required the application of new mean-
ings and interpretations not anticipated by the developer,"[15] writes
Missouri attorney Marvin J. Nodiff.

If circumstances change, rules and restrictions should, too. Associations should constantly review their restrictions to ensure they are
current (see pages 67–69).

2. Does it create safety hazards? Most courts will choose safety
over aesthetics—and reasonable community associations recognize this.

In 1993, a Massachusetts couple placed safety netting around
their balcony. The netting was installed to prevent their 16-month-
old son from slipping through the railing and falling to the parking
lot below. The bylaws prohibited alterations to the common areas,
however, and the board voted 3-1 to remove the netting. Then the
board reexamined its decision. Board members claimed they misun-
derstood the purpose of the netting, believing it was for privacy, not
safety, and allowed the couple to keep it. The board even named the
child's mother as chair of a new balcony committee.[16]

Risking a child's safety for architectural integrity is not logical—
and a court would likely feel the same way. Associations need to be
flexible—and reasonable—in matters involving safety.

Other associations haven't learned this. In 1995, the *St. Louis Post-
Dispatch* reported on Sameh Al-Malt, a six-year-old boy in Chesterfield, Missouri. Sameh is autistic, mentally retarded, hyperactive, and
diabetic. Three times, according to *Post-Dispatch* columnist Christine
Bertelson, Sameh slipped between openings in a neighbor's fence and
jumped into their swimming pool. Because of his abilities as an es-
cape artist, the Al-Malts wanted to build a six-foot fence in their
backyard. The Baxter Ridge homeowner association refused. It only

allowed four-foot fences. The couple asked for an exception; the board still said no, despite letters from the mayor of Chesterfield, the Judevine Center for Autism, and St. Louis housing authorities. The association changed its position only when faced with a $5,000 fine for violating the Fair Housing Amendments Act of 1988.[17]

Even without the Fair Housing Act, this association's actions seem unreasonable. What is more important—uniform fences or a little boy's life?

The safety issue is less clear when dealing with security devices. Should a board allow a security system that violates the covenants—such as window bars or high-watt lighting—or should it enforce the covenants and potentially jeopardize a resident's safety? In the 1991 case *Hawkins* v. *Jamaicaway Place Condominium Trust*, Stephen Hawkins asked several association directors about installing security bars on first-floor windows. Based on the association documents and the Massachusetts Condominium Act, the board told Hawkins that security bars were an improvement requiring approval. It told him how to obtain approval, but he never followed through.

Shortly thereafter, Hawkins' wife was raped. The couple sued, claiming the association was liable. Both a lower court and an appeals court ruled in favor of the association, noting that the Hawkins could have put the bars on the inside of their windows. "It was wholly within the Hawkins' ability to protect themselves," wrote the court.[18]

An association shouldn't disregard residents' security, however. According to Seth Emmer, a community association attorney in Braintree, Massachusetts, boards should probably permit security devices, but try to minimize the aesthetic impact.

"A board's overall purpose is to ensure the health and safety of the unit owners," said Emmer, "not just to enforce the covenants."[19]

3. Is it unenforceable or too intrusive? In Honolulu, Hawaii, the Kukui Plaza condominium association had a rule banning candles. The rule required "electric illumination" in units, making Kukui Plaza a "no candles" condominium. While the association had good intentions—reducing the risk of fire—the rule seems nearly impossible to enforce (unless the association formed an elite squad of candle snuffers). A rule such as this will likely be considered unreasonable. To its credit, the association ultimately eliminated the ban as part of an exhaustive review of the community's rules and regulations (see page 69).

A rule isn't the answer to every problem. Avoid enacting rules, as one attorney put it, that attempt to "stop every act of human stupidity." Candles may be fire hazards, but that doesn't mean it's reasonable to ban them.

4. Does it allow alternatives? In August 1995, a Calabasas, California homeowner association began enforcing a long-standing policy against skating in the street. The rule applied to roller skates, in-line skates, skateboards, and street hockey. According to the *Acorn* newspaper, violators faced a $50 fine for the first offense and $25 for future violations.[20]

On the surface, this seems like an unreasonable rule. Telling residents they can't skate in the streets is similar to saying they can't walk in the streets. Yet this association offered alternatives. Skaters were still allowed to skate on sidewalks, driveways, and patios. More importantly, the board designated one parking lot as a skating zone.

Inflexible rules are unreasonable rules. Associations should provide residents with options. Instead of banning Christmas decorations, allow decorations from Thanksgiving through New Year's Day. Instead of prohibiting tool sheds, allow sheds in backyards if they aren't visible from the street. Be flexible.

5. Does it unfairly target a particular group? Rules and restrictions that unfairly benefit a majority of residents at the expense of a minority, or create two classes of residents, are typically not reasonable. In 1995, a North Carolina appeals court ruled that an association's user fee was invalid, since only renters were forced to pay it (the fee was charged to renters who use the community's recreational facilities).[21] Twelve years earlier, a Baltimore circuit court ruled that an association parking regulation was unreasonable since it favored resident owners over nonresident owners.[22]

Why were these rules unreasonable? According to attorney David H. Fishman, they bestowed "an economic benefit to one group of unit owners to the unfair exclusion of another group of unit owners."[23] And as these cases show, a rule can be unreasonable not only by favoring a majority, but by unfairly favoring the board of directors. In the Baltimore case, a grandfather clause gave each board member more parking spaces than other residents.

Discriminatory restrictions also are prohibited by state and federal laws. The most significant of these laws is the **Fair Housing Amendments Act of 1988.** The Fair Housing Act prevents discrimination against any person in the sale or rental of a unit—or in using a community's services or facilities—based on race, color, religion, sex, or national origin. Associations should avoid any hint of discrimination in these categories. A resident in a Pennsylvania condominium charged his association with religious discrimination under the Act for scheduling its 1997 annual meeting on the first night of Rosh Hashanah, a Jewish holy day. When the Rivers Bend III Condominium Association refused to reschedule the meeting, the resident filed suit seeking an injunction to stop the meeting. Although the judge did not grant the injunction, he urged the association to avoid such "insensitive" scheduling conflicts in the future.[24]

In 1988, Congress added a provision to the Act prohibiting discrimination in housing based on familial status or handicap. (The term "familial status" means one or more individuals under the age of 18 who live with a parent or legal guardian.) The Act affects community associations in the following ways:

■ *Familial Status*—Under the Act, it is illegal for community associations to discriminate against families with children. This means that any rule specifically targeting children—such as prohibiting small children from using a community swimming pool— could be illegal (see section on children, pages 42–43).

The Act also addresses occupancy restrictions. According to Atlanta attorney George E. Nowack in his article "Full House," the Act allows reasonable limitations on occupancy, as long as they aren't discriminatory. The U.S. Department of Housing and Urban Development (HUD) has stated that reasonable occupancy requirements—based on factors such as the number and size of bedrooms and the overall size of the unit—would comply with this exemption. But HUD has also held that when investigating discrimination complaints based on familial status, it would carefully examine occupancy restrictions to determine whether they unreasonably limit or exclude families with children.[25]

Defining family is not as simple as it seems. The U.S. Supreme Court, in the 1995 case *City of Edmonds* v. *Oxford House*, ruled that the city's occupancy restrictions violated the Fair Housing Act. The city claimed that Oxford House, Inc., which had opened a group home for 10 to 12 recovering drug addicts and alcoholics, violated a single-family occupancy ordinance limiting the number of people who could live in a home unless related by blood, marriage, or adoption. It was an ordinance similar to community association occupancy restrictions. The problem was its strict definition of family, which violated the Fair Housing Act. That means restrictions against group homes, halfway houses, and other care facilities probably violate the Act as well.

HUD continues to struggle with occupancy restrictions. As of 1998, it had approved resolutions limiting occupancy to no more than two persons per bedroom, said Nowack. Occupancy restrictions cannot be based on the relationships of the parties—restrictions cannot require occupants to be related by blood, adoption, or marriage. Any attempt to limit occupancy other than by the number of persons per bedroom is unreasonable. (Issues such as this that affect the fundamental use of the property should be dealt with in the governing documents, not by passing a rule.)

"It appears that community associations can limit the number of persons—roommates—that occupy a unit, so long as they don't discriminate against families with children or handicapped persons," wrote Nowack. "If associations want to establish occupancy restrictions, they should rewrite their documents to remove any definition of a 'single family.' " If an association wants to restrict the number of roommates that can occupy a unit, added Nowack, the restriction should state the maximum number of occupants allowed and note that it does not apply to handicapped persons or families with children. "Such a restriction may not be exempt, but it shows the association had no intent to discriminate."[26]

Age restrictions are prohibited by the Act as well. To qualify as an adults-only community—defined as "housing for older persons" in the Act—a minimum of 80 percent of an association's unit must be occupied by at least one person age 55 or older. The community also must publish and adhere to policies and procedures demonstrating intent to provide housing for seniors.

▌ *Disabilities*—The Act allows persons with disabilities, at their own expense, to make reasonable modifications to a property to accommodate their needs. An association that refused to allow these reasonable modifications would be charged with discrimination.

Massachusetts attorney Seth Emmer notes that this provision attracted little attention when the Act was passed. That's partly because HUD's examples were straightforward. For example, if parking were available on a first-come, first-serve basis, a person with a disability should receive preference. Similarly, a blind person with a seeing-eye dog may not be denied occupancy or use of the common areas and amenities because of a no-dog restriction. But most cases involving reasonable modifications have not been so clearly defined.[27]

According to Emmer, a modication is considered reasonable if it is feasible and practical under the circumstances. It is unreasonable if it entails undue financial hardship or administrative burden.

"Associations must respond to these requests with understanding and compassion," writes Emmer. "Associations should, where feasible and practical, accommodate *bona fide* requests and accept the burden, unless it is unduly expensive or not feasible. No association, however, must succumb to outrageous demands. Unreasonable requests and unreasonable behavior need not be tolerated."[28]

Associations also must contend with the **Americans with Disabilities Act** (ADA)—a civil rights statute that prohibits discrimination against people with disabilities. Under Title III, which focuses on public accommodation, disabled persons must be able to access public places, such as restaurants or stores. For community associations, public accommodations would include any service or facility open to the general public, such as a pool or clubhouse, depending on its use.

The primary distinction between the ADA and other federal and state acts, said Janet L.S. Powers, an attorney in Irvine, California, is that the association bears the costs of modifying a building or common area.[29]

Writing Reasonable Rules

Most boards write rules rather than covenants. Covenants are based in the original documents and can be changed only through amendments, which require owner approval. Rules can be passed by board resolutions. When writing and enacting rules, boards of directors should follow these five steps:

1. **Determine if a rule is necessary.** First, identify the problem. What type of activity or behavior is creating complaints? Is it a community-wide problem or is it isolated? If the problem is limited to one person, you may not need a rule.

Unfortunately, many directors fail to ask these questions. Many associations enact rules when they may not be necessary—or reasonable. Just because a resident plays his guitar on the balcony doesn't mean the association should ban musical instruments, or that musicians should not be allowed outside.

"If an actual problem exists, the board should address it," writes Katharine Rosenberry. "It is generally unwise, however, to create a rule simply because one neighbor is posing a problem."[30]

As Gurdon H. Buck notes in CAI's *GAP Report #7—Drafting Association Rules*, personality conflicts, design defects, and miscommunication often create problems that can be resolved without a rule. Writing a rule should be a final solution. A board should try alternative solutions first, such as simply talking to neighbors who are entangled in a dispute. Sometimes people aren't even aware they're creating a problem.[31]

2. **Conduct research.** To determine if a rule is the *right* solution, the board should conduct research. It should review the governing documents and make sure the board has the authority to adopt the rule and the tools to enforce it. It should also ensure that a similar rule hasn't already been passed.

When writing a rule, involve the association attorney. Ask the attorney to review the rule's wording and to ensure that it is legal and enforceable.

3. Involve residents. Residents should have a role in establishing rules, since they're the ones who must live by them. Association members, for example, need to decide the types of animals they wants as pets. The decision should not be made by one board member who has an aversion to rabbits.

The Sentinel of Landmark, a 272-unit condominium in Alexandria, Virginia, revised its pet rules in 1996 through the efforts of its pet committee. The committee, which consists primarily of pet owners, spent two years revising the rules, and led an effort to amend the bylaws. The pet owners ultimately decided that residents could have one dog per unit and two cats—no one decided it for them. The committee now addresses all pet-related complaints.

According to Florida attorney James P. Curry, involving residents when rules are created—through surveys, meetings, or other means—minimizes future enforcement problems.

"Give the people every chance to be heard, a chance to put it to a vote, and they'll go along with it," said Curry. "There is a lot more resistance when a board makes a rule without telling anyone. Then people ask, 'why is this suddenly illegal? I've been doing this for years.' "[32]

4. Be specific. Rules should be clear. A vague rule will be open to a variety of different interpretations. Many court cases result from ambiguous rules. If a rule is specific, it will be easier for residents to understand and easier to follow.

Consider pet rules. If you were training a dog, you wouldn't tell Fido, "Desist in engaging in the motion of all four paws and legs." You'd say "down." Or "sit." Or "stay." The same principle applies to association pet rules. Whether for dogs, cats, or parakeets, association rules should be clear and well-defined.

"Don't just say that pets are permitted," said Sue Carpenter, PCAM, a long-time Florida community manager. "Say what types are permitted and how many. If there are certain types of animals the community doesn't want, be specific."[33]

When the Sentinel of Landmark revised its pet rules, it included

12 general rules, such as "Pets shall not be left unattended outside the unit or in a vehicle." The rules also list the following activities as nuisances:

■ Pets running at large, except in the two designated dog-run areas
■ Pets damaging, soiling, defecating on, or defiling any private property or the common elements
■ Pets causing unsanitary, dangerous, or offensive conditions
■ Pets causing noticeable odors
■ Pets making or causing noises of sufficient volume to disturb any resident
■ Pets attacking or otherwise interfering with the freedom of movement of persons and other pets on the common elements (including designated dog-run areas), chasing vehicles, attacking other pets, or creating a disturbance in any other way

All association rules should be specific. Consider home business restrictions. According to Maryland attorney Thomas C. Schild, restrictions need language more specific than just "no businesses." Instead, use language such as "The following activities shall be deemed to constitute business activities…"

"If things are clearly going to be prohibited, be specific," said Schild.[34]

5. Communicate the rule. Association rules, both new and old, should be consistently communicated to members. Publicize rules in the newsletter at least once each year. Give new owners "Welcome to the Community" packages that include rule information. Publish a rule book and distribute copies to members. Publicizing rules not only makes residents aware of them, it also helps them understand their purpose.

"Joe Homeowner may be adamant about bringing his wonderful, obedient dog to the pool," writes attorney Jay S. Lazega. "However, if Joe knows that a dog could lead the health department to fine the association and close the pool, he would be more likely to comply with the regulation."[35]

CHAPTER TWO

Reasonable Enforcement Strategies

"Overzealous boards are
typically the most dangerous problem
when enforcing covenants."

—*Ross Feinberg, attorney
in Newport Beach, California*

Enforcing rules and restrictions can be a good way
to lose friends. Neighbors must tell neighbors that
their fence is too tall, their driveway too wide, or
their garden too big. Boards are sometimes forced to levy
fines, suspend privileges, and file lawsuits. Sometimes it's
the only way to gain compliance.

"A lot of times, boards don't want to rock the boat if
the owner refuses to comply," said Hawaii attorney Richard Ekimoto in the *Common Ground* article "A Board's Best
Friend?" "But in many cases, if the association fails to
consistently enforce a rule, it can lose the right to enforce it in the future."[1]

Many boards have the opposite problem. They're
overzealous. They enforce restrictions like a dictator
crushing a rebellion. They fail to hold hearings. They levy
fines before owners can correct the violation. They are

opposed to alternative dispute resolution techniques, such as mediation. They enforce a rule simply because it's on the books—even if it
doesn't make sense.

When enforcing rules and restrictions, the board's goal should
not be to punish an owner, but to gain compliance. Reasonable enforcement procedures recognize this.

Confirm the Violation

When Helen Garrett was charged with "kissing and doing bad
things" in a community parking lot (see page 7), one of the
association's worst mistakes—among many—was accusing her of a
violation she didn't commit. Associations must always confirm the
facts in a violation case. According to Virginia attorney Denise
Palmieri, the board must know exactly what happened, when, where,
and who observed the violation. Complaints from neighbors should
be submitted in writing—this, said Palmieri, avoids changing stories
or failing memories. It can also make owners less inclined to complain.

"Identify which specific rule or part of the documents has been
violated," writes Palmieri in an article on hearings. "Be critical in ana-
lyzing the violation—a judge is likely to put your analysis to a test
and you want to look reasonable."[2]

Proactive or Reactive?

How an association discovers violations can be as controversial as
how it enforces them.

There are two ways to go about this. One way is a "proactive"
approach. With this approach, the association regularly inspects
homes for violations. If violations are spotted, residents are notified.
According to proponents, this is a more consistent method of enforcing rules and covenants, and it treats everyone fairly. The other
method is a "reactive" approach. Instead of periodic inspections, the
association acts on complaints from residents. The board then inves-
tigates these complaints and provides due process to violators.

Which method works best is a source of some debate. Pat
D'Avanza, CMCA, manages several communities for Shea Manage-

ment, Inc., in Bethesda, Maryland. She believes that "reactive" enforcement procedures—relying on neighbor complaints—are more damaging to a community than proactive enforcement. Owners at odds with their neighbors will abuse the system. Those charged by the association will wonder why they were singled out.

"Owners who receive violation notices based on this random approach respond with charges of harassment or capricious imposition of rules," wrote D'Avanza. "This scenario leads to a McCarthyesque pattern of investigation."[3]

Some homeowners claim inspections are equally McCarthyesque. Seven years ago, the Reston Association—a 20,000-unit planned community in Reston, Virginia—considered a mandatory inspection program. But some residents protested bitterly. So Reston relies instead on a complaint system. The association still conducts some inspections, however. To meet a disclosure requirement under the state property owners act, it inspects homes for sale for violations. Architectural control staff also conduct inspections at the written request of subassociations.

"Residents are informed three to six months in advance," said Steve Jacobson, covenants outreach coordinator. "Our goal is to gain compliance, not to penalize [owners]."[4]

So which method works better? Proactive or reactive?

"I don't know that there is a correct legal answer," said Ekimoto, a CAI trustee. "If I were a board member, I'd probably act on complaints or information obtained naturally by the association. It's important that an employee or board member act when they do come across a violation. But I think the most important thing is for the association to be consistent."[5]

Washington, D.C. attorney Benny Kass believes "a very conservative proactive approach—walking the community for junk vehicles, boat trailers and oversize trucks—is acceptable."[6] The problem is when associations become overzealous, and neighbors begin spying on neighbors. That, said Kass, can lead to abuse of power.

Kass makes the following recommendations to associations that take a proactive approach:

■ If permitted by your association documents, have the membership elect the members of the architectural control committee.

■ If the board appoints these members, circulate an announcement to all owners, inviting them to participate.

■ If the board decides to pursue a proactive enforcement policy, inform the entire membership. A straw poll at the next annual meeting also is a good idea.

■ Wherever possible, make sure two people inspect any alleged infractions—preferably one committee member with the manager.

■ Respect your neighbors' privacy. Do not sneak around in the middle of the night with a flashlight and binoculars.

■ Document your case. Take pictures where appropriate of any alleged violation. Obtain permission if you take pictures on the inside of property.

■ Make sure the manager and all committee members read and thoroughly understand the legal documents. Consult the association attorney if there is any doubt about what the association can and cannot do.

"As legal counsel for many associations, I am all for enforcing the legal documents," Kass writes. "However, if a committee is walking around houses, looking into windows, searching and hunting for violations, this is not acceptable and may, indeed, be actionable."[7]

Informal Contact

Sometimes residents aren't even aware that they're violating a restriction. That's why attorney James P. Curry believes the best way to start the enforcement process is with a casual conversation.

"The first contact should be informal," said Curry. "Some boards start an enforcement case with a letter from the lawyer to show they mean business. This just annoys most people. The associations that treat first violations informally seem to have fewer problems."[8]

Consider the case of the Minnesota hot tub. In 1993, the *Common Ground* article "Playing by the Rules" told the story of several college-age men who lived in a townhome community in St. Louis Park, Minnesota. The unit was owned by the father of one of the residents. Neighbors already were complaining about noise when the men in-

stalled a hot tub on their patio—which violated the association's nuisance rules. When the men refused to comply with the rule, the
board gave their neighbors the father's phone number. Whenever
they were bothered by noise, they called dad. Shortly thereafter, the
tub was gone.

"A friendly reminder—in person or in writing—will often resolve
most rule violations without the need for more formal hearings,"
writes Palmieri. "Be sure to send a friendly person to deliver the message, however. Sending the most abrasive board member to 'set this
guy straight' will defeat your goal."[9] Some attorneys suggest sending
a witness as well.

Be Consistent, But Flexible

An unreasonable board is usually inconsistent. Boards cannot prohibit
commercial vehicles and then allow the board president to own a
Weinermobile. It cannot ignore a rule for six years and then suddenly
decide to enforce it. "Directors should utilize business judgment with
every violation," said attorney Ross Feinberg. "No violation should be
completely ignored."[10]

Procedures should be consistent, too. If an owner ignores the board's
friendly reminder to comply with the restrictions, the association should
send the owner a written notice of the violation. According to F. Scott
Jackson, a violation notice should identify the restriction, the specific
reasons for the violation, and "provide the member with a time and
method for curing his or her noncompliance."[11] It also should inform the
owner of potential penalties—such as fines and possible legal fees—
and the procedures for requesting a hearing. Owners should be given
time to correct the violation.

If the owner still fails to comply, send a final notice asking him or
her to appear at a hearing. Check with your association attorney—
some states have specific requirements regarding hearing notices.

Remember—the goal is compliance. Try to help residents. Offer
assistance if they need clarification. Include contact names and
phone numbers. Let them know that the association is not a secret
police force, but a group of neighbors who are willing to help.

Grandfather Clauses and Time to Comply

Some associations include a grandfather clause when writing new rules. If an association passes a restriction banning pets, for example, a grandfather clause allows residents who already own pets to keep them for the remainder of the pet's life. This shows that an association is flexible and sensitive to the hardships caused by a new restriction. Some attorneys, however, argue that grandfather clauses create more problems than they solve.

"People may think it's okay to violate the rule," wrote Denise Palmieri in the *Common Ground* article "Take Your Time." "If a board allows blue shutters, then prohibits them with a grandfather clause, new owners may move in, paint *their* shutters blue, not knowing that they are against the rules."[12]

But some CAI members disagree. "The board must be mindful of the hardship that rule changes may impose on the homeowners," wrote a *Common Ground* reader in response to the article. Another reader added: "Immediate enforcement of a new rule seems somewhat cruel, and can often cause psychological financial pain to residents."[13]

One option is to give owners a reasonable amount of time to comply with new rules. Every new rule, said Palmieri, should include time for adjustment. And if an owner is cited for an existing rule, reasonable associations will provide time to correct the violation.

"My procedure is to err on the side of generosity," said community manager D. Raymond Faucher, PCAM. "If you wind up in court and haven't given someone time to turn a situation around, the courts may not look strongly upon your position."[14]

Providing Due Process

Community associations are democracies. And in any democracy, those accused of crimes—or in this case, violating rules or restrictions—should be able to defend themselves before a jury of their peers.

That's why community associations should hold hearings. Hearings give homeowners charged with a violation the chance to tell their side of the story and to defend their position. A hearing also shows that the board is fair. As Palmieri notes, hearings allow the board to obtain all of the facts in a case, which leads to more logical, more reasonable decisions. And if the case proceeds to trial, a court will look more favorably on an association that provides due process than one that arbitrarily enforces the rules.[15]

"The best hearings are those that determine the facts in a case, not punishments," writes Palmieri. "[Is the purpose] to bring neighbors together to discuss the impact of certain behavior on the community and to encourage compliance with the rules? Or is the purpose of the hearing to punish and shame a rule violator?" [16]

Palmieri offers the following tips for running business-like enforcement hearings in her *Common Ground* article "Do You Have a Hearing Problem?"

Determine who should hold a hearing. Check the governing documents. The declaration may authorize only the Covenants Committee to hold hearings. If the documents are silent on this issue—and many are—the board may need to adopt procedures. Regardless of who holds it, the hearing should be impartial. It should not be conducted by the homeowner who submitted the complaint.

Begin the hearing on time. Start the hearing at the time stated in the notice and hold it even if the owner fails to participate. Upon hearing the evidence, you may find that—even without the owner's response—there isn't enough evidence. Don't just assume a violation exists—a court won't.

Identify the participants. Identify everyone participating in the hearing or simply observing it. Wouldn't you like to know if the man in the back is the owner's lawyer or a reporter?

Explain the process. Before the hearing begins, explain how it will work, how much time has been allocated, and how participants will be notified of the results. Read the notice of violation and the applicable rule so that everyone knows what the hearing is about.

Act business-like. Dress and act as if this is a business meeting. This means no chit chat or joking. Some associations hold hearings in a law office to add a sense of formality.

Be impartial. Any interested members of the hearing panel should excuse themselves from the hearing. The complaining owner, for example, should not sit on the panel. The panel should discuss only matters that are relevant to this specific violation—rumors about the defendant, for example, are irrelevant.

Present both sides. Allow the participants to present evidence and to ask questions. The panel should also ask questions so it obtains the information it needs to make a decision. It should not, however, engage in accusations or hostile contact with the participants.

Make the decision. The panel should dismiss the participants when making its ruling. If possible, it should make the decision immediately following the hearing, unless further facts or verification are necessary. Although it is sometimes best to spend a few days on a well-written decision, the longer the issue remains unresolved, the less likely the decision will reflect the facts. The exception is if the hearing is charged with emotions. In this case, the panel may want to allow a cooling-off period before making its ruling.

Be reasonable. Make the ruling reasonable. Will a court approve of a $500-per-day fine for cooking odors? Probably not. Issue the ruling promptly and avoid over-explaining it.[17]

Mediating Disputes

Sometimes litigation is necessary to enforce rules and restrictions. But associations that sue their neighbors often pay a high price, both financially and emotionally. Lawsuits tend to drag on for years, dividing communities and draining finances. The damage can outweigh the benefits, particularly for petty disputes over dog doo or basketball hoops.

These high costs are one reason why many associations are turning to alternative dispute resolution (ADR) techniques. ADR is any procedure used as an alternative to litigation. The best known of these procedures are mediation and arbitration. According to the American Arbitration Association, mediation is a process in which parties submit their dispute to a third party (the mediator) who helps them reach a nonbinding settlement of their dispute. Arbitration is similar, but the settlement is binding, and a third party makes the decision. In several states, ADR is required for resolving certain types of disputes.

Its success rate is impressive. Vivian G. Walker, Ph.D., an authority on ADR, notes that through mediation alone the odds are eight-to-one that two parties will reach a mutually satisfactory agreement. And this success comes much cheaper and much faster than through litigation. According to David Norvell, a community association manager and a mediator for the San Diego Mediation Center, some nonprofit organizations or local governments offer mediation services for free. Private mediators often charge from $25 to $250 for a session.[18]

Low fees aren't the only benefit. Unlike lawsuits, where one side wins and one side loses, mediation is less combative.

"Association disputes lend themselves so well to mediation," said Leland Chang, executive director of the Neighborhood Justice Center in Honolulu, which operates a state-financed community association dispute resolution service. "You're talking a lot about relationships that need to be put back on a positive track. People are going to continue to live with each other, so any kind of an adversarial process just causes problems to worsen. With mediation, there is a healing that doesn't happen in any other process."[19]

Levying Fines

You can beg residents to follow the rules, you can threaten them, *plead* with them, yet sometimes only one thing gets their attention: money. That's why many community associations use fines to enforce rules and covenants. If a homeowner parks in the wrong spot, fine him $25. If an owner hangs a flag, fine her $15 a day until she takes it down. People get the message fast: play by the rules or pay.

Unfortunately, fining is an extremely negative way to deal with a problem. It puts community associations in the role of the unhappy parent, punishing the disobedient child.

Treating neighbors like kids and breaking into their piggy banks is not a great way to build community. Boards that levy fines should consider these tips from the *Common Ground* article "Go to Your Room!":

Establish a policy. Associations should issue fines only after giving residents every opportunity to correct a violation and after providing due process.

A New Jersey appeals court confirmed the wisdom of that statement in 1994. The case involved the Briarwood Condominium Association and resident Jane Walker, who was moving out of the 96-unit building. Her son and son-in-law helped her move and parked a truck on the lawn in front of the building. That violated the rules, so the association fined her. Because her son brought his dog, she was fined for that, too.

Walker sued. A lower court ruled in her favor, stating that the association issued the fine without sufficiently investigating the violation or providing due process. The Appellate Division of the state Superior Court not only upheld the decision, it found that neither the governing documents nor state law provided the board with the power to fine. (The New Jersey legislature rectified this by amending the state Condominium Act in 1996.) [20]

The Briarwood case also sent a message about reasonability. According to many experts, the court was not pleased by the association's overzealousness in fining Walker without a hearing or without any offer of due process.

Fines should not be levied based on the whims of the board. Assuming the board has the authority to fine residents, it should develop fining policies that cover everything from what they cost to when they are levied.

A reasonable fining policy requires the association to notify the owner of a violation before levying fines. Some board members prefer to talk with the owner first, to see if the matter can be resolved. At some point, however, the owner should be contacted in writing. Attorney Beth Grimm, chair of CAI's California Legislative Action Committee, believes this notice should include these points:

∎ The nature of the violation
∎ A realistic time limit for correcting the violation
∎ The fine (or schedule of fines) to be imposed if the violation is not corrected
∎ Information on the owner's right to a hearing

"Associations should bend over backwards to give due process and be reasonable," said Michael Pesce, PCAM, former chair of CAI's New Jersey Legislative Action Committee. These procedures also must be uniform and must apply to all members.

Fines should be considered only when all other steps have failed. If the association provides due process, and if the owner still does not correct the violation, the association can generally exercise the power to fine.

The violation should fit the fine. There is no magic formula for setting reasonable fine amounts. The best rule—assuming that fine amounts aren't regulated by state law—is that the less serious the offense, the lower the fine. Most courts disapprove of associations that fine residents $300 a day for hanging a bird feeder. The purpose of the fine is to correct the violation, not to raise funds for the association.

"I've had boards say fines should be included in the budget, but this essentially tells owners we want them to violate the rules so we can make a few dollars," said Pesce. "The point of the fine is to stop the violation."

Courts have shown their distaste for fines that unreasonably accumulate. A California association fined an absentee owner $100 each time he used the community amenities. Over time, the fines grew—with interest—to $5,465. The owners sued the association in 1995 and won over $400,000 in damages.

"A lot of associations let fines pile up because they think they're not collectable," said Pennsylvania manager Edward J. Golob, Jr., PCAM, who has taught a CAI seminar on fining. "Then they're shocked when they get in court and find they've jeopardized their position by allowing the fines to grow to such large amounts."

Golob suggests that associations go to court or mediate to collect fines once they total $300. Most attorneys recommend collecting fines through small claims courts, though this can be time consuming. Which raises a question: is fining even worth the time and trouble? In a 1995 *New York Times* article,[21] Maryland attorney Steven Silverman expressed his disdain for fines. Courts, he said, usually allow only minuscule fines, rendering them useless—it is easier for residents to pay a small fine than to correct a violation. Silverman believes the threat of legal action makes a stronger impression on violators.

Others, however, believe a world without fines would make life difficult for associations. "Fines at least bring compliance in some cases. They're a deterrent," said Pesce.

One alternative is to suspend privileges—to cut off access to amenities like the pool until a violation is corrected. While this can provide strong incentive to correct the situation, enforcement can be difficult. "If you deny the use of the swimming pool," said Golob, "who is going to stand at the gate?"

The problem with suspending privileges is also similar to the problem with fines—they place volunteer directors in the role of disciplinarian parents. That's why fines must be levied with care. Boards should give owners time to correct the violation and the opportunity to appear at a hearing.[22]

Making Exceptions

Not enforcing a rule or restriction is like not answering a ringing phone—it feels uncomfortable. After all, if an owner breaks a rule, the association is compelled to enforce it. A rule's a rule, right?

"There is no law that says you have to enforce the rules for every violation," said Ross Feinberg, an attorney in Newport Beach, California. "If an infraction has no impact on the purpose of the association, don't enforce it. The key is simply to document the decision."[23]

Feinberg uses sheds as an example. If a covenant prohibits sheds, and an owner builds a shed in his backyard where it can't be seen, there's no reason to enforce the covenant. The shed is invisible—it has no impact on the community. That one exception does not mean, however, that another owner can put a red aluminum shed in his front yard.

Some attorneys believe exceptions are a bad idea. Len Siegel, a California attorney who defended the no-pet restriction in *Nahrstedt v. Lakeside Village Condominium*, believes most association restrictions are reasonable and enforceable. Making exceptions, he says, invites a certain amount of risk.

"If a board has fully investigated the enforceability of a restriction, and determined that enforcement would not be appropriate, it can make a decision not to enforce it," said Siegel. "But it can be a risky proposition. It can result in claims of selective enforcement. It can possibly nullify the restriction for future enforcement." [24]

There's also risk in enforcing rules that have no effect on the association. And if an exception is documented, it will nullify the "selective enforcement" charge.

"An association is not going to lose the right to enforce its rules because it didn't enforce an illogical restriction," said Massachusetts attorney Stephen Marcus. He adds that most association documents contain nonwaiver language. In essence, an association that waives a restriction does not waive it against another owner (or if there's an additional violation by the offending owner).

"People have stopped looking at the objective of a rule, and are enforcing for the sake of enforcement," said Marcus. "For over 20 years this has been our way of thinking—if you make an exception, you'll lose the rule. I think courts are starting to say that this makes no sense." [25]

Boards need to distinguish between infractions that are technical violations and those that truly affect the value or safety of the community. If there is no rational reason to enforce the restriction, the board needs to carefully document its decision and explain why it chose—in this one case—not to enforce the restriction. Here are three steps for making exceptions: [26]

Determine the violation's effect on the community. When a resident breaks a rule or violates a covenant, the board must determine its effect on the community. How do you measure this? According to Feinberg, the board must consider the association's purpose, as defined in the governing documents. Typically that purpose is to maintain the community and to preserve property values. Then the board must ask itself: does the violation have a direct effect on the purpose of the association? Will it create a nuisance, such as loud noises or toxic smells? Will it significantly alter the appearance of the community? Will it create a safety risk? Is the violation even visible? Will enforcing the restriction violate federal or state laws?

Consider home business bans. If an owner runs a home business that can't be detected, it makes little sense to enforce the restriction. But if an owner is repairing refrigerators in his garage, with parts scattered through the yard and large trucks making frequent stops, enforcement seems more logical. The board can reasonably argue that the business is hurting the community and creating a safety risk.

Make a business judgment. Once the board has determined the violation's effect on the community, it must make a business judgment. A business judgment should be the result of investigation and consideration of facts. Feinberg believes a business judgment that will be upheld includes three traits: (1) the judgment was made in the best interest of members, (2) the association acted in good faith, and (3) it consulted with professionals to reach the judgment. It allows the board to say it relied on the advice of experts to make what it determined to be the correct decision, if its decision is questioned.

"More and more courts are applying the business judgment rule to community associations," said Stephen Marcus. "The trend is to not second guess a decision, even if it's wrong, if the board acted in good faith." [27] But courts are still grappling with the concept, said Marcus. Consider *Riss* v. *Angel*.[28] Board members, in a case involving an architectural approval clause, claimed they were protected from personal liability by the business judgment rule. The Washington Supreme Court said that even if the rule did apply, "the board's failure to adequately investigate would remove it from the rule's protection."[29]

Document decisions. Good documentation is essential when granting exceptions to rules and restrictions. Some attorneys suggest that boards record the decision-making process in meeting minutes; others recommend a resolution stating why the violation did not warrant board action. However it is recorded, the board's explanation should be as detailed as possible. It should outline why the board made an exception and how the decision was reached.

Feinberg recommends a system he calls PASS: list the Purpose, Authority, Scope, and Specific occurrence. Why, for example, did the board grant an exception? What was its authority? Does the decision apply to all of the members? To one of the members? What specific occurrence caused the resolution to be drafted? Whether the board decides to enforce the restriction or to waive it, it should notify the owner of its decision.

CHAPTER THREE

Controversial Rules and Restrictions

"After consulting with Geoffrey, I
have been advised that there are
many cats loose in Piney Lakes and
we are not at all certain that the cat
'clawing at screen doors, doing
damage, and creating a nuisance' is
my client."

—*1977 letter from a cat's attorney to a community association*

No matter how reasonable your rules are, or how reasonable your enforcement procedures may be, certain rules and restrictions will cause controversy. Kids, pets, flags, Christmas decorations—these are emotional issues, and restrictions that confront these issues generate emotional responses.

Here are some sources of controversial restrictions and ways to deal with them.

Children

W.C. Fields once said he'd never met a kid he liked. In some communities, judging by the rules they pass, Fields must serve on the board of directors.

A Florida condominium association passed a rule in 1995 that prohibited children from playing outside. The board claimed that injuries to children on common areas could lead to higher insurance claims, higher rates, and expensive lawsuits. Opponents said that insurance concerns were a poor reason for an unreasonable rule.

"You don't have more liability because kids are playing outside," said Fred Buehle, staff attorney for Broward County's Human Rights Division, in a Ft. Lauderdale *Sun-Sentinel* story. "That's like saying kids can't live on the second or third floor of a high-rise because they might fall off a balcony. It's just a pretext to regulate the conduct of kids."[1]

It could also be a potential fair housing suit. An Illinois condominium passed a rule prohibiting children from riding bikes on sidewalks, skating, playing ball in common areas, and skateboarding. If a child was caught breaking these rules, the families would be fined $100. Residents and a local housing agency filed a fair housing complaint with HUD in 1995, which resulted in a settlement. According to the Tinley Park *Star*, the agreement allowed all residents to use the common areas for recreational purposes. It also required the association's manager to attend a fair housing seminar.[2]

Prohibiting children from playing outside is unreasonable. Reasonable alternatives include the following:[3]

▮ Provide tot lots and recreational facilities—give kids a place to play
▮ Install modern, interesting equipment—make sure kids are attracted to the play area
▮ If skateboarding or rollerblading are creating unsafe situations, educate parents of the dangers through meetings and the newsletter
▮ Invite a medical expert or a police officer to discuss these dangers at the annual meeting
▮ Develop a list of areas (local parks, for example) where skateboarding and other activities are permitted

Unreasonable pool rules will also attract the attention of HUD. George E. Nowack, in his article "Full House," cites three cases in which seemingly innocuous pool policies were found to discriminate against families with children:[4]

■ A homeowner association in Florida required children age 10 or under to be accompanied by an adult in the pool. Children under five were not permitted in the pool at any time, and children aged five to 16 were only allowed in the pool from 11:00 a.m. until 2:00 p.m.

■ A Hawaii association with identical swimming pools labeled one an adult pool, the other a family pool.

■ In metropolitan Boston, a condominium association required a rest period of 10 minutes every hour for children under the age of 18 and established times for adults-only swimming.

Why are these rules discriminatory? According to Nowack, pool rules must protect the health, safety, and welfare of the child. Rather than barring small children from the pool, pool rules should require all users—not just kids—to have swimming skills. Use restrictions should not give special privileges to any age group. Rules and restrictions that are more restrictive for children than adults are probably unreasonable and illegal.[5]

Flags and Flagpoles

Disputes involving the American flag follow a familiar pattern. First, a patriotic resident—usually a veteran—erects a flagpole in his yard or flies a flag from the front of his house. The community association, which prohibits flagpoles, flags, or other outdoor decorations, orders the resident to remove the flag. The resident has never heard of the rule and simply ignores it. When the association levies fines, the resident ignores those, too. The resident then calls the local newspaper, which runs an outraged story about the communist community association and the courageous veteran.

Numerous flag flaps have followed this pattern. In 1996, a North Carolina veteran and his wife ignored three judges' orders to take down a flagpole that violated a restriction against "masts, towers, poles, or antennas." They complied only when threatened with 15 days in jail for contempt of court. In 1994, a Las Vegas association ordered a couple to remove their flag or face a $500 fine. (The association's letter was dated June 14—Flag Day.) That same year, a California association threatened to fine a resident for flying the flag—which he said he'd flown for 20 years on patriotic holidays, such as Independence Day.[6]

The resident also raised a legitimate question: will an American flag *really* hurt property values?

It depends on the community. Some residents object not to flags but to flagpoles. Others say that flapping flags make too much noise. The key, as always, is to be reasonable. Consider allowing residents to hang flags on certain holidays, such as Independence Day and Veterans Day. Consider banning flagpoles but allowing flag brackets on units. Survey residents and learn their feelings on flags. (Some states, such as Delaware, have passed legislation guaranteeing unit owners the right to fly the American flag.)

An association can provide alternatives without compromising its position. At a Virginia Beach condominium in 1992, a retired Navy veteran covered the front of his unit with a large flag. The flag violated the covenants; the owner had not requested permission to hang it. According to Brad Brady, PCAM, whose company Community Group managed the condominium, the association offered the owner a number of alternatives. It offered to install a community flag pole. It offered to let the owner hang the flag on the back side of the unit. It offered to survey residents about the flag restriction. The owner did not accept any of the offers and community opinion shifted to the side of the association.[7]

Holiday Decorations

It's as much a holiday tradition as trimming the tree. Each year, at least one community association becomes entangled in a dispute over Christmas lights. In 1996, a California condominium ordered residents to remove Christmas decorations, citing safety concerns and a bylaw provision against outdoor attachments.[8] In 1995, a West Covina, California association threatened to take down an owner's decorations and charge her for the costs.[9] In 1994, an Illinois association threatened an owner with $5,000 in fines for hanging Christmas lights.[10] And just to prove that decoration disputes aren't confined to Christmas, a Florida homeowner association ordered a resident in 1996 to remove her Halloween decorations.[11]

So do Christmas, Halloween, and other seasonal decorations—even when hung in abundance—truly cause property values to plummet?

"I personally don't believe that somebody who decorates for holidays affects property values," said *Common Ground* contributing editor Brian Erickson, CMCA, PCAM. Erickson is community manager of the Great Northwest Community Improvement Association in San Antonio, Texas, a two-time winner of CAI's Community Association of the Year award. "One could even argue that holiday displays suggest a sense of community, neighborliness, and fun that could make an area more desirable."[12]

Christmas and other holiday decorations can place a board of directors in an uncomfortable position, however. Some decorations could create safety hazards. Virginia attorney Raymond Diaz and Ohio manager Rick Edelman, in the 1993 article "Christmas Covenants," agree that residents should not be climbing the sides of buildings or placing themselves in dangerous situations in common areas. If residents are injured, the association could be held liable.[13]

But most safety issues can be addressed without banning decorations entirely. If an association is concerned about safety, it could ask residents to not overload electrical circuits. Or, the association could require lights rated for outdoor use. Edelman suggests that associations ask residents to use electric decorations with the Underwriters Laboratories seal. Requiring that lights be turned off by a certain hour—10:00 or 11:00 p.m.—lowers the risk of fire while the community sleeps. The association could remind residents of these safety tips in the newsletter before the appropriate holiday.

Decorations in common areas are another source of controversy. Associations often complain about damage from nails and staples. Then there's the fear of liability. What happens if a resident falls off a ladder while decorating a commonly owned wall? One way to avoid this without being a Scrooge, said Ellen de Haan, is to make decorating common areas a community effort.

"Decorating common areas is not easy in a condominium setting, since virtually everything outside the unit is common elements or limited common elements," she said. "In a community that wants to decorate, I suggest forming a committee to take care of the common areas. If funding becomes an issue, sometimes owners will donate lights and decorations."[14]

While protecting common areas is a concern, aesthetics are the primary reason for decoration restrictions. Some people may love decorations, but others think they're gaudy. And without restrictions, some residents may keep their blinking 20-foot Santa in their yard until June.

What's the reasonable approach? As with most aspects of common-interest living, the association must determine what its members want. Five years ago, a Fairfax, Virginia condominium association ordered a tenant to take down his Christmas lights. An association rule prohibited residents from attaching anything to building exteriors, trees, or shrubs—including any yuletide decorations. Faster than Santa slides down the chimney, the association was scrutinized by the local media and portrayed in newspapers and on TV as "would-be Grinches." The board, feeling trapped in a no-win situation, allowed the tenant to keep the lights through the holiday. The next month, the association held a public meeting. The board wanted to learn what residents thought about the rule against decorations. Should the rule be changed? Should it even exist? Most residents said they did not want the buildings damaged and they did not want Christmas lights scattered throughout the community. As a result, the rule stayed on the books.[15]

If an association wants to restrict holiday decorations, it must be reasonable. Most courts will probably not support an all-out ban on holidays decorations. Allowing decorations with certain limitations *is* probably reasonable and is far more likely to stand up in court—and to be supported by residents. An association that wants to maintain decorations standards, said de Haan, must carefully evaluate its goals. Then it must write rules that realize those goals in a reasonable fashion, with a minimum of bad feelings and a maximum of good judgment.

Time limits can be one way of pleasing both sides. A time limit would allow owners to keep up lights or other decorations for only a certain amount of time—for example, from Thanksgiving through early January. This prevents one of the biggest complaints about decorations: the resident whose plastic Santa is still outside on the fourth of July.

"We try to use common sense in addressing this kind of thing," said Erickson, whose community does not have specific restrictions on holiday decorations. "If your Christmas lights are still up by the middle of February, we probably will ask you nicely to put them away."[16]

The key is to ensure that the association doesn't become over-zealous, or its restrictions unreasonable.

"Sometimes common sense gets lost in the fervor over these disputes," said Erickson. "I'm afraid we may end up with so many specific rules and regulations that you'll need a lawyer to know if you can put up your lights. It's a time for celebration, isn't it?"[17]

If you don't agree—if you believe that holiday decorations *can* diminish a community's appearance—ask yourself: what hurts property values more? Holiday decorations that hang for three weeks, or an association so unreasonable, so inflexible, that it bans them altogether?

Home Businesses

In Murrieta, California, a 77-year-old violin teacher sold her home in a gated community after violating a covenant against home businesses.[18] In Clackamas, Oregon, a piano-teaching couple faced similar covenants before they even moved into the neighborhood.[19] In St. Louis, a homeowner association filed suit to stop an owner from teaching piano.[20]

Each of these cases occurred in the summer of 1996. And each case involved the same complaint: that home businesses—in this case music lessons—create too much traffic.

George E. Nowack believes it's a legitimate complaint. To determine if a home business is a nuisance, Nowack's firm recommends a test. If you can see, hear, or smell a home business, it's probably a nuisance. The firm recently added a fourth condition: a business is also a nuisance if it draws an unreasonable number of clients to the property.[21]

Music teachers can certainly violate this condition. Nowack once dealt with a teacher who gave 75 lessons a week, which meant 75 cars entering and exiting the community. Other communities have faced similar problems. An Arizona planned community enforced home business restrictions against a 81-year-old woman selling Avon after neighbors complained about delivery trucks. David Swedelson, an attorney with Swedelson & Gottlieb in Beverly Hills, California, represented an association with a homeowner who ran a refrigerator repair shop from his garage. With people constantly dropping off refrigerators—and workers noisily making repairs—the business was an obvious violation of the covenants.

These outward appearances are important. According to Maryland attorney Thomas Schild, courts look at the volume of customer traffic, employee traffic, noise emanating from the unit, the hours of operation—"If there is no intrusion or interference with other people in the quiet enjoyment of the use of their property, it's more of a technical violation," said Schild.[22]

Home business restrictions become unreasonable when they violate Nowack's four conditions—when a business can't be seen, heard, or smelled, or it doesn't increase traffic. Consider a day-care business. A day-care operator working out of the home, undetected, is not a problem. But if numerous cars are entering and exiting the community, if the business owner allows the children to use association facilities, such as the pool—which could create liability risks—or if the children begin damaging property, the board has a problem.

"The whole concept is intrusion into the neighborhood," said Nowack. "You'd never know an accountant is working out of a unit, which is why blanket 'no business' restrictions are unreasonable. But if that accountant's clients start driving in and out of the community, that's an intrusion."[23]

Landscaping

You'd think landscaping disputes would only occur when owners ne-glected their yards. If they only cut their grass in odd-numbered years. Or if they planted something so atrocious—hedges cut to look like Don King—that community property values plummeted.

But community associations frequently become snarled in dis-putes with owners trying to *beautify* their yards. In 1994, Elfriede Kristwald and her Georgia homeowner association became tangled in a thorny dispute over roses. Kristwald developed a plan to put rose bushes, decorative bricks, and a birdbath in her front yard. The RoseWalk Homeowner Association in Atlanta ruled against her plan, claiming it violated the covenants.[24] One year earlier, a California su-perior court judge ordered an owner to remove 5,000 rose bushes he'd planted in his yard and pay his homeowner association $35,000 in legal fees. His work was only half done—the owner planned to plant 10,000 rose bushes in all. But the association claimed the plantings were leading to tree cuttings and improper grading and drainage work. The bushes also were planted in straight lines, which violated association rules.[25]

Roses aren't the only source of landscaping disputes. In 1996, a Florida couple planted 19 trees in the front yard of their Coral Springs home. Their association said the owners did not receive ap-proval for the trees—most of which were palm trees—and that the landscaping was inconsistent with the community. It also said the ex-cessive trees hurt property values and home sales, provided hiding spots for criminals, and invited termites and other pests. The associa-tion eventually filed suit to obtain removal of the trees.[26]

That same year, in Palm Harbor, Florida, two teenage brothers grew a 20-foot long, 16-inch wide vegetable garden near a hedge behind their townhome. The boys washed cars to pay for their top-soil and seeds; their mother said it helped them cope with the death of their father. But their association saw things differently. On Christmas Eve 1995, four months after starting the garden, the family received a letter telling them to remove it. The board main-tained that the garden violated a provision against "mass plantings."

Neighbors wrote the association to express their approval of the garden.[27]

So how can a reasonable association avoid such seeds of discontent? First, by writing clear rules. "Mass plantings" is not clear. What is a mass planting? How would you define "mass?" The association should determine whether such rules are even necessary. In this case, the garden was behind the home. And a large percentage of owners did not support the rule.

"Enforcement should be reserved for those violations that have an impact on association living," said attorney Ross Feinberg. "When a board procures a reputation 'condo commandos' out to enforce every rule, the substantive violations become much more difficult to enforce."[28]

Outdoor Play Equipment

Swingsets and basketball hoops, like manicured lawns, are part of the suburban landscape. Yet many community associations have restrictions against outdoor equipment. Some people think that swingsets are ugly. They complain that basketball hoops are unattractive or noisy.

"Portable" basketball hoops are a frequent source of problems. A portable hoop seems like a reasonable alternative: owners can still have a driveway basketball hoop; because they're portable, they aren't permanent structures. The problem, however, is when "portable" becomes "permanent." Some residents grow tired of dragging the hoop from the driveway and leave it there for months. Others find the portable hoop isn't as portable as they thought.

A California Superior Court addressed this issue in 1996. Homeowners Benjamin and Marcia Milchiker had replaced their garage basketball hoop with a portable hoop. The garage hoop violated the Nellie Gail Ranch Owners Association's governing documents. Unfortunately, the Milchikers failed to move the portable hoop out of sight each night, so the Laguna Hills, California association filed suit.

"The Milchikers testified that the 'portable' hoop was too heavy to move," said Stanley Feldsott, the association's attorney, in the July/

August 1996 *Common Ground*.[29] If something is too heavy to move—the hoop structure weighed about 400 pounds—it probably isn't portable. But in March 1996, Superior Court Judge H. Warren Siegal ruled that the Milchikers could keep the hoop, claiming that the association's rules only applied to hoops attached to homes, not to portable hoops.

Does that mean you can't require owners to store portable hoops when they're not using them? Not at all. The Wagon Wheel Canyon Community Association in Orange, California, contains the following requirement in its architectural guidelines: "Portable, free-standing basketball backboards are permitted, provided they are removed on a daily basis and when not in use. In no event shall [they] be visible from the street, sidewalk, or community property when...not in use." The association has had few problems with compliance.

Some associations allow residents to keep portable hoops outside for longer periods. In mid-1997, a Northern Virginia association allowed an owner to leave a portable hoop outside in the summer, assuming he put it away in the winter.

"The association decided to live with the portable basketball goal," said the association's attorney, Wil Washington. "Their documents simply didn't prohibit a temporary item like a portable goal and the board didn't want to duke it out in court."

A Miami, Florida association didn't want to duke it out with its owners either. So when 30 percent of the membership asked the board to reconsider its portable hoops policy, the board agreed. Howard J. Perl, AMS, PCAM, the association's manager, said the board now allows residents to store portable hoops outside under certain conditions:

- No permanent poles are allowed in the ground
- All hoops must be stored no more than halfway down the driveway
- Residents cannot play basketball in the street
- The hoop must be kept in good condition and must not damage landscaping
- Owners must request permission for the hoop from the architectural control committee

▌ Any common area grass damaged because of the hoop must be repaired at the owners' expense

The association reserves the right to rescind its approval of the hoop—after first sending a violation notice and holding a hearing—if the hoop creates a nuisance, such as traffic disruptions and noisy midnight basketball games. The guidelines, once approved by the board, were mailed to all unit owners.

According to Perl, of Continental Group, Inc., in Miami, the association adopted the policy for a simple reason: it's what members wanted. Previously the association had fined a number of residents for leaving portable hoops outside overnight. A group of concerned owners convinced the board to send a survey to members. The survey, said Perl, showed that many owners were willing to allow hoops under certain conditions.

Surveys are invaluable tools when making emotional community decisions. That's why the California Summit-Aliso Viejo Association sent its members a portable basketball hoop survey. At the time, the association had not passed rules regarding portable hoops. The survey offered residents the following choices:

▌ Basketball units should be allowed for use in the driveway and stored completely out of sight when not in use

▌ Basketball units should be allowed for use in the driveway and stored on the driveway or the side of the home with the approval of neighbors and the Architectural Review Committee

▌ Basketball units should not be allowed at any time

The surveys were tabulated and discussed at the association's monthly board meeting in January 18. Based on the results, the association now allows portable hoops, provided they are stored out of sight when not in use.

Some associations still allow residents to mount basketball hoops the old-fashioned way—on top of the garage. Wagon Wheel is one such association. It allows residents to mount backboards on garages, though it prohibits driveway backboards mounted on poles. Its architectural guidelines require the following:

▌ Residents must obtain the approval of the association's architectural review committee before installing a garage backboard or a free-standing backboard in backyards or side yards

- Backboards must be centered on the garage roof and above the garage door
- Backboards must be painted to match the trim or stucco of the house
- Backboard supports must be painted to match an adjacent surface
- Residents cannot allow the net to become shredded or "otherwise fall into disrepair"

"I think these are clear, fair guidelines," said Jan Harrison, PCAM, president of Action Property Management, Inc., which manages the Wagon Wheel association. "We use these as a successful model in many of our communities."[30]

Swingsets can also cause controversy. In 1993, a family built a three-story play structure—complete with ladders, a playhouse, bridge, and tower—in the backyard of their California home. Neighbors complained that the structure was too big. One neighbor even planted trees to block it, without success. The association cited the couple for violating its covenants, and for not including the height when it submitted its architectural plans.[31]

In this case, it's easy to see why the association acted. The structure was visible from other homes, which could affect property values.

A Maryland association was less reasonable. Because the common areas lacked a swingset, Bruce and Vivienne Elliott wanted to build one in their backyard. The couple asked their community association for specifications, but the association said it did not allow swingsets. Ultimately, the Maryland Human Relations Commission filed a lawsuit against the association, claiming it discriminated against families with children.[32]

This association seems unreasonable. Why ban swingsets from backyards if they're not visible?

"When faced with the installation of outdoor equipment, boards should first determine if this equipment is prohibited by use restrictions in their documents," said Ross Feinberg in "Spring Fever, Covenants Blues," a 1994 *Common Ground* article. "If such a restriction exists, the impact of the installation must be weighed in order to

determine whether or not to take enforcement action."[33] As an example, said Feinberg, a side-yard single swing would be far less ob-
jectionable than a front-yard sports court. "Ask yourself: would I, as a
homeowner, want to live across the street from this equipment?," said
Feinberg. "The differentiation then becomes clearer."[34]

Paint Colors

Most association covenants limit the colors that owners can choose
to paint their units. The reason is simple: to prevent owners from
painting their homes colors that may hurt property values, such as
bright pink or fluorescent gold. The problem, however, is that owners often fail to read those covenants, then paint their home an unap-
proved color. Or, the color they choose looks far different in the
paint store than it does on their home. In September 1993, for example, Dave and Donna Hammond painted their Eagle River single-
family home a bright sky blue. The Hammonds admitted the color
was much "bluer" than they expected. It also clashed with the soft
earthtones of their neighbors' homes. The couple never submitted
the color to their association's architectural committee, and ultimately the association ordered the couple to repaint the house or
face a $500 fine.[35]

A reasonable association tries to prevent these problems by
clearly publicizing the architectural control process in its newsletter.
It also communicates which colors are approved by the association.

At the Highlands Ranch community in Highlands Ranch, Colorado, the association maintains a notebook of paint samples. The
book contains a variety of color schemes to help residents choose
paints; it also identifies base, trim, and accent colors. Residents who
select one of these pre-approved color schemes do not have to wait
for Architectural Committee approval.

The association also keeps a book of potentially problematic colors. If an owner is considering a color that may be too bright, a staff
member can usually find a comparable color in the book. Then, he or
she can show the owner a home with a similar color scheme.

"I often ask, `Do you want your house to be brighter than that?'

Usually they didn't realize how bright a house would look with their sample color," said Karen Black, architectural control manager.

Black's model was the architectural control program at the nearby Ken-Caryl Ranch association in Littleton, Colorado. At Ken-Caryl, paints are categorized in notebooks based on base color. Each color book contains samples, brands of paints, paint numbers, and addresses of homes painted with that color.

"That way, you can really show someone what a color looks like," said Black. "Those tiny paint samples look a lot brighter when they're up on a house."[36]

Paint colors leave less room for compromise than other association regulations. An odd paint choice can disrupt a community's carefully planned color scheme. This can lead even the most reasonable associations to court.

In 1991, the English Hills Homeowner's Association in Redmond, Washington filed suit against two owners, Mr. and Mrs. Leroy Jones. In 1989, without the approval of the English Hills Architectural Control Committee, the Joneses painted their house light purple with an eggplant accent and teal trim. Several neighbors complained about the colors, which contrasted with the development's earth tones.

The association tried to be reasonable. Before filing suit, English Hills began arbitration proceedings with the couple. The two sides reached a binding agreement. The agreement acknowledged the association's authority to restrict paint colors. It also stated that the couple would submit colors to the architectural control committee for approval, repaint the house if required, and pay the association's attorney's fees if further court action was necessary. But at the last minute, the Joneses refused to sign the settlement. So the association sued. Ultimately, after a three-year court battle in which the association garnished the Joneses' bank account—and after the couple refused the association's final offer—the judge gave the couple a deadline to agree to a new color scheme. The penalty if they failed: a $2,000-a-day fine and a possible jail term. The couple also was ordered to pay the association's $13,000 in attorney's fees.

According to Kris J. Sundberg, the association's attorney, community associations must take their covenants seriously:

> The board of directors, if no one else, must have a
> clear understanding of the restrictive covenants,
> their purpose, and what can happen if they are not
> enforced. There are many people…who have never
> read the covenants or don't think they apply to
> them. If the board does not understand the basic
> concepts inherent in the covenants—the protection
> and enhancement of property values—and the ne-
> cessity of covenants enforcement, you will get at
> best only haphazard compliance and enforcement.[37]

Pets

Pet restrictions can be one of the most controversial issues faced by a board of directors. For many pet owners, their dogs and cats aren't simply "pets"—they're friends and companions. Enforcing restrictions, even reasonable ones, can be problematic if not handled properly.

"Restrictions on noise and smells, prohibitions on commercial breeding, compliance with leash and license laws, and requirements that owners clean up after their pets are all reasonable," said Honolulu attorney Richard Ekimoto.

More troublesome restrictions include the following:

Weight restrictions. Many associations restrict pets based on their size. "No pets over 25 pounds are allowed." "Owners may not keep dogs taller than two feet at the shoulders." These types of rules can be problematic. Yes, they allow residents to have dogs. But is it reasonable to evict a dog that weighs 26 pounds? And a size limit, be it weight or height, doesn't eliminate many of the problems associated with pets. A Schnauzer is just as likely to bark as a Doberman Pinscher.

"I don't understand the logic of weight restrictions," said Colorado attorney Ed Burns. "What types of problems are created by small dogs, but not big dogs? Both of them bark. Both foul the common areas. I can't identify what a weight limit solves."

Proving the correct weight can also be difficult. In 1992, a home-owner association in a Florida community accused an owner of keeping a dog that violated its 30-pound weight limit. The case went to court. The two parties took the dog to an animal hospital, accompanied by their attorneys and a court reporter. When they put the dog on the scales, he wouldn't sit still. The scales tipped between 29.4 and 31.5 pounds.

An additional problem is that a dog's weight isn't necessarily stable. In Mangonia Park, Florida, a resident found a puppy—a German shepherd mix—under some bushes following Hurricane Andrew. The association prohibited dogs over 20 pounds; when the resident found the dog, which she named Andrew, and began caring for him, Andrew didn't violate the rule. Then, he grew to 43 pounds. In 1994, the association told her that the dog would have to go—two years after she first brought Andrew to her unit.

To avoid that problem, the Sentinel of Landmark condominium in Alexandria, Virginia based its 50-pound weight restriction on information from the American Kennel Club (AKC). The AKC offers guidelines on dog breeds and the average weight of these breeds as adults. That way, if an owner wants to buy a labrador retriever puppy, the association can show that the puppy will weigh more than 50 pounds in about six months.

Pet bans. New home buyers thought that pets were allowed at the Society Hall at Galloway Township II condominium in New Jersey. Many existing residents owned dogs themselves. But in 1991, the association had passed a resolution banning pets. In 1995, it tried to enforce it.

You can't enforce a rule—particularly a total ban—that you've ignored for four years. If an association bans pets, it needs to ban them completely. It can't prohibit pets except for Mrs. Smith's cat, which the directors try to ignore. The *only* exceptions are those pets required by handicapped or disabled persons.

"Seeing eye dogs and signal dogs (for the hearing impaired) are required under the Fair Housing Act," said Ekimoto. "Some cases have ruled that if someone is emotionally disturbed and they need a

pet to cope, you have to permit the pet." Other exceptions not man-
dated by law, said Ekimoto, are more difficult. It's possible to include
a provision in the documents allowing the board to grant exceptions
for hardship cases. The problem is defining a hardship. In Lake
Worth, Florida, for example, a resident had cancer surgery. Her
daughter moved in with her mother in mid-1996 to take care of her,
and brought her dog. Unfortunately—now here's a surprise—her
mom lived in a no-pets building. And when the dog began spotting
the common areas, neighbors began to complain.

   "My feeling is that an exception needs to be twofold," said Burns.
"There has to be a legitimate medical need and the animal must be
specially trained to meet that need."

   You also need to enact the ban through an amendment to whatever document—the declaration or bylaws—that permits the association to regulate a unit's interior. According to Gurdon H. Buck, the
Uniform Common Interest Ownership Act, which has been adopted
in some form by 23 states, makes it clear: if a person's private dwell-
ing space is affected, the unit owners must consent to an amendment
of the declaration to impose a use restriction on that area. Before enacting a rule that affects the interior of a unit, carefully review the en-
abling statute.

   Courts have occasionally overturned no-dog rules. In 1996, an Illinois appeals court, in the case of *Board of Directors of 175 East Delaware
Place Homeowners Association* v. *Hinojosa*,[38] ruled that the association's ban
on dogs was unreasonable. The ban was unduly burdensome, said the
trial court, because the association could have written restrictions to
control pets rather than banning them outright. (The court eventually reversed itself, however. The association argued that the court
had examined the wrong part of the Illinois Condominium Property
Act in reaching its decision. The court had stated that the association
couldn't simply write a rule banning pets—it needed to amend the
declaration. But the association's attorneys noted that Section 18.4
(h) of the Act gives boards the power to adopt rules and regulations
"to promote orderly living on the property." That reversal led
Carlson—a former board member—and her husband to appeal to the

Supreme Court, even though they no longer live in the building and their dog is no longer alive.[39])

Rules and restrictions aren't the only way to resolve pet problems. If you want pet owners to pick up pet poop, for example, make it easy for them. Some associations buy pooper scoopers and dispensers for storing them in common areas. Others buy boxes of sandwich bags or encourage residents to use grocery bags. Probably the best way to reduce pet waste problems is to give dogs a place to play. That's why many associations create dog runs—fenced-in areas with trash cans where dogs can run without a leash.

It also means confronting pet owners. If a resident sees an owner whose dog likes to howl until sunrise, he or she should say something. If a manager spots an owner while his dog is spotting the common areas, he or she should say something. The key, said Burns, is to be direct, to be specific, and to be patient. "When you talk to people, say, 'This is the problem,' instead of 'Hey! We have a rule and you're breaking it!' Explain the problem and let them know why it needs to stop."[40]

Satellite Dishes

Satellite dishes used to be huge. They were large enough to receive signals from Mars. In those days, bans on satellite dishes usually made sense. Now, however, many satellite dishes are 18 inches in diameter. They can be disguised as rocks, tables, and patio umbrellas. Does a total ban still make sense?

The answer is no. The question, however, is somewhat irrelevant. Section 207 of the Telecommunications Act of 1996 directed the Federal Communications Commission (FCC) to write regulations prohibiting restrictions that "impair a viewer's ability to receive video programming services." The FCC did just that, adopting a final rule that became effective October 14, 1996.

The FCC rule prohibits associations from unreasonably restricting television antennas, satellite dishes less than one meter in diameter (except in Alaska, where the rule covers DBS antennas of any size), and multipoint distribution service antennas less than one meter in size (with towers less than 12 feet above the roof line). It applies only to property where a resident has direct or indirect ownership and exclusive use or control. In meetings with CAI, FCC staff has also stressed that the rule applies to limited common area locations like decks, patios, and balconies in condominiums and cooperatives (though the FCC may treat co-ops as being entirely common property).

Associations may still restrict all other antennas. An antenna restriction is valid unless it:

▌ Impairs reception of an acceptable quality signal

▌ Unreasonably prevents or delays installation, maintenance, or use of an antenna

▌ Unreasonably increases the cost of installing, maintaining, or using an antenna

An association restriction must meet each of these conditions or it will be considered invalid.[41]

In 1997, the FCC finally offered some guidance on the types of restrictions prohibited under the rule. As part of the rule, the FCC allows anyone—associations, owners, tenants, local governments—to file a Petition for Declaratory Ruling. This is a process for determining whether an antenna restriction is valid. By early 1998, the FCC had issued rulings on eight petitions. In each case, the FCC ruled that the restrictions in question were invalid.

The rulings show how the FCC interprets the rule. Among the lessons associations must learn:

Any prior approval, application, or permit process is not allowed. In issuing its ruling on July 22 in the case of *Star Lambert* v. *City of Meade, Kansas,* the FCC ruled that the city's permit and $5 application fee caused unreasonable delay and expense. It also ruled that the permit and fee could be a disincentive for potential antenna users.

Any permit fee is an unreasonable cost increase. Similar to the *Star Lambert* case, a prior approval process and $5 fee were overturned in the case of *MacDonald* v. *Savannah Lakes Village Property Owners Association.* The FCC will not allow any permit fee, regardless of its size.

The burden of proof is on the association. In the case of *Lubliner* v. *Potomac Ridge Homeowners Association,* one of three rulings is-

sued by the FCC on October 14, petitioners Jay Lubliner and
Deborah Gavlin, claimed they could not get adequate reception by
placing their TV broadcast antenna in their attic. Instead, it needed
to be put on the roof. Potomac Ridge argued that its regulation was
enforceable as long as the indoor antennas received acceptable quality signals. The FCC disagreed, claiming the association had not met
its burden of proof by testing and establishing the reception quality
from the petitioner's attic. As this order makes clear, the FCC intends
to strictly apply the burden of proof requirements to associations.

Antenna users have an "absolute right of placement." The only
exception is if there are safety or historic considerations. In the case
of *MacDonald* v. *Savannah Lakes Village Property Owners Association*, the association claimed an approval process was needed to protect paleo-
Indian remains on and near the association. These remains, the association argued, made the community eligible for inclusion on the
National Register of Historic Places. This would also exempt the association from the FCC rule.

The FCC rejected this argument, since the association had provided no proof of National Register qualification. The FCC reiterated
that prospective antenna users have an "absolute right of placement ab-
sent safety or historic preservation considerations." (Owners, however,
must comply with association placement specifications, unless those
specifications violate one of the conditions mentioned on page 60).
Other lessons include:

■ Any restriction must provide exceptions to compliance for unreasonable delay in antenna installation, maintenance, or use; unreasonable cost increase for antenna installation, maintenance, or use; or
preclusion of acceptable quality signals

■ To qualify for the rule's safety exception, the safety rationale must
be clearly articulated in the antenna restriction[42]

Associations can still restrict antennas in certain ways. Honolulu
attorney Richard Ekimoto, who helped write CAI's formal comments
on Section 207, states that associations can do the following:

Require screening. Assuming they meet the rule's three conditions, associations can require residents to screen antennas. Screening

is anything, such as a plant, that makes the antenna less obtrusive. Associations can also require owners to paint antennas. However, if a rule is stricter for antennas than for other outdoor equipment, it may not be enforceable. An example would be a rule requiring owners to paint their satellite dish but not their air conditioning unit. (The FCC was expected to issue a ruling on this in early to mid 1998.) The primary requirement is that screening cannot unreasonably increase the cost of video programming services. "If an owner accuses an association of unreasonably increasing his or her costs," writes Ekimoto, "the FCC will examine the cost of the system and service, then the cost of the screening, and determine whether they are reasonably proportionate."[43] A screening cost is more likely to be reasonable if the antenna is obtrusive and the resident pays a large monthly service fee. (Again, associations must always consider the three requirements on page 60.)

Request less visible placement. Associations can require residents to place antennas in locations where they are less visible, said Ekimoto, such as backyards or side yards. But the same conditions apply as with screening: the placement cannot impair the signal, unreasonably delay installation, or unreasonably increase the cost of installation. "The most common problem with placement—as well as with screening—will be in determining if a resident receives an adequate signal,"[44] said Ekimoto.

Prohibit antennas on common property. The FCC antenna rule does not apply to common or rental property. When it released the rule in August 1996, the FCC asked for additional information. It wanted to investigate the feasibility of allowing individual antenna installations on common or rental property without the association's permission.[45] As of March 1998, when this book went to press, the FCC still had not released a rule on common property. Until that rule appears, community associations *can* prohibit antennas on common property. As mentioned, the FCC rule applies only to property where a resident has direct or indirect ownership and exclusive use or control. It also applies to limited common area locations such as decks, patios, and balconies in condominiums or cooperatives.

Associations and their attorneys should review their documents to ensure they comply with the FCC rule.

Signs

In 1991, a Florida couple placed a sign stating "Buyer Beware" in the window of their condominium unit. Their association was not amused and sued them for violating the restrictive covenants. Shortly thereafter, Judge William T. Blackwell ordered the couple to remove the sign and to refrain from posting it in the future. Although they took down the sign from their unit, the couple then placed magnetic signs on their car stating "Buyer beware of Naples Winter Park I" and drove the car on condominium property. A judge found them guilty of contempt, ordered them to perform 100 hours of community service, and placed them on probation for 90 days. When they refused to perform the community service or to meet with their parole officer, the judge sent them to jail for 30 days.[46]

Jail time for hanging a sign? Doesn't the First Amendment of the U.S. Constitution guarantee the right of free speech?

Yes and no. The First Amendment applies to "state actions"—actions taken by a local, state, or federal government. Community associations are private organizations; therefore, the First Amendment does not apply. As attorney Mark D. Imbriani writes, "There is nothing constitutionally impermissible *per se* in a private agreement regarding signs in a planned residential community."[47]

A 1996 Pennsylvania decision supports this opinion. The case, *Midlake on Big Boulder Lake Condominium Association v. Cappucio*,[48] arose in 1989 when the Cappuccios placed two for-sale signs in the windows of their unit. The signs violated the condominium's declaration, which required prior written permission to post signs. The board asked the homeowners to remove the signs, but they refused. The association sued; the Cappuccios claimed they had a right to post the signs under the First Amendment's guarantee of free speech. In 1995, a Pennsylvania trial court ruled in favor of the Cappuccios.

An appeals court reversed the decision. It ruled that the First Amendment does not apply to the enforcement of private covenants.

The court also rejected the notion that community association rule enforcement is the same as state action. As a result, the First Amendment did not apply.

That doesn't mean associations should ignore the Constitution, however. "Associations should be cognizant of constitutional rights and make every possible effort to ensure that such rights are honored and protected," write attorneys Paul G. Skalny and Susan R. Rapaport, in their *Common Ground* article "Sign of the Times."[49]

Jonathan Woolf-Willis, a California attorney, offers the following advice for reasonably enforcing sign restrictions:

▌ Avoid total prohibitions. A restriction that totally bans residential signs may be overly broad and unenforceable.

▌ Limit restrictions to physical characteristics. In the 1994 Supreme Court case *City of Ladue v. Gilleo*,[50] the court noted that the physical characteristics of signs can be regulated. This is an important guideline for associations as well. In adopting sign regulations, associations should focus on factors such as size, location, the number of signs, and the amount of time the sign can be visible.

▌ Don't base restrictions on content. Residents should be free to determine what content any message will have in a properly displayed sign. The only limitations are on obscene or illegal messages.

▌ Offer alternatives. Residents are more likely to follow restrictions if the association provides alternatives. For example, rather than instituting a total ban on window signs, the board could limit sign displays to first floor windows only or to one central location.[51]

Vehicles

Certain types of vehicles—jalopies, dump trucks, 18-wheelers—are not terribly attractive. They also take up precious space in tight community parking lots. That's why many community associations have vehicle restrictions, typically against commercial vehicles, recreational vehicles (RVs), campers, and inoperable vehicles.

The problem is that many of these restrictions are blanket restrictions. They ban all types of vehicles, regardless of their particular circumstances. Many associations, for example, have blanket restrictions against trucks. While the intent was to prevent residents from parking mack trucks, delivery trucks, or construction vehicles, associations frequently interpret this to include pickup trucks, too. Some courts have upheld such restrictions; others have not.

"Community associations with broad 'no truck' restrictions should explain in a board resolution how they will handle different types of trucks," said attorney Ross Feinberg in the *Common Ground* article "Car Trouble."[52] This means considering a truck's commercial characteristics, such as its engine size, height, length, weight, and whether it includes any signs. By doing so, an association can clearly and objectively define the types of trucks it will allow.

The same principle works for restrictions against RVs, campers, and travel trailers. Rather than base decision on hard-to-define categories, size limitations are clearer and less vague.

"There's little ambiguity about whether a vehicle is in violation if it exceeds the size limitation stated in the association's restrictions," said Arizona attorney Don Dyekman.[53]

Reasonable alternatives are also helpful. If the community has space, it should set aside an area where residents can park large vehicles. Likewise, said Dyekman, some associations allow residents to park RVs and boats in their backyards as long as they aren't visible from neighboring properties. Other associations allow large vehicles as long as they're screened behind trees, bushes, or fencing.

Reasonable restrictions will also avoid outright bans against commercial vehicles. The intent, obviously, is to keep out vehicles that look like billboards on wheels. But not all commercial vehicles are a threat to property vehicles. In 1994, a Florida association ordered resident Ed Davis to remove a commercial vehicle from his driveway.[54] Davis is a police officer; the vehicle is a police car. Is that really a commercial vehicle? Isn't a police car a deterrent to crime? Likewise, if an owner parks a commercial vehicle in his garage, thereby keeping the vehicle concealed, isn't it illogical to enforce the restriction? What about commercial vehicles with company lettering on the sides? Will that *really* hurt property values?

"Legally, community associations can allow commercial vehicles with exterior signs and still prohibit commercial vehicles with equipment,"[55] Feinberg said. Associations can pass a general resolution documenting how it will enforce its commercial vehicle restrictions. That way a community association can permit vehicles with company lettering—or whatever the community is willing to allow—without being accused of selective enforcement.

Motorcycles are another source of controversy. In 1993, the board of managers at the Jefferson Village Condominium in Yorktown Heights, New York amended the association's bylaws to prohibit motorcycles (for both owners and visitors). Ronald Nuzzo, who was the only motorcycle owner in the adult community—and who moved there before this ban was passed—filed suit. A trial court voided the ban, but the appellate division of the state supreme court declared that the ban was within the board's authority. Because Nuzzo failed to prove misconduct, fraud, or conflict of interest on the board's behalf, the court could not review the ban's reasonableness.

"Motorcycle bans don't make sense in this day and age," said Eric Lundquist, legislative affairs specialist for the American Motorcycle Association (AMA), which paid Nuzzo's legal fees. "If associations are going to make restrictions based on noise and safety, [the restrictions] should apply to cars as well. There's no reason to treat motorcycle riders differently."[56] Feinberg agrees. "People have a right to transportation licensed by the government," he said. "Unless the use or repairing of a motorcycle constitutes a nuisance or an eyesore, you can't disallow that right."[57]

As with most rules and restrictions, it's a good idea to survey the community. Hal Barrow, a Pennsylvania attorney, suggests in his *Common Ground* article "Are Parking Lots Strictly for Cars?" that associations ask residents what kinds of vehicles they think should be permitted.

"Don't be surprised by the responses and suggestions," writes Barrow. "What's important is that you obtain the input of your neighbors, and that your neighbors have a chance to give it. Once the board makes its decision, homeowners will be more likely to comply with the new rules, and the board will be in a stronger position to enforce them legally, if need be."[58]

CHAPTER FOUR

Eliminating Unreasonable Rules

"An association is not going
to lose the right to enforce its rules
because it didn't enforce
an illogical restriction."

—Massachusetts attorney Stephen Marcus

J ust because a rule or restriction is on the books doesn't
mean it's reasonable. It also doesn't mean that residents are aware of it—or that they support it.

"The board is not responsible for blindly enforcing every provision in the documents," writes Missouri attorney
Marvin J. Nodiff. "Instead, the board has discretion to *not*
enforce a specific provision, particularly when it may be
illegal and expose the association and the owners to financial or criminal penalties."[1]

The board also has a responsibility to periodically review the rules and restrictions. And if they are outdated or
unreasonable, the association should discard or rewrite
them. Here are some ways to ensure that restrictions are
reasonable and supported by the community.

Listen to the Community

If residents object to a restriction, listen to their reasons. In 1996, the Courts of Four Seasons Homeowners Association in Annapolis, Maryland had planned to file suit against owner Thomas S. McMahon. McMahon's fence violated two covenants, the board charged, and needed to be moved back eight feet. But at an association meeting, many residents said they thought legal action was unnecessary. They later supported this position by circulating a community petition.

The board responded to resident concerns. Three months after voting to sue, it voted 3 to 2 to offer McMahon a compromise. McMahon, who said he could not afford to go to court, accepted. Under the agreement, McMahon moved his fence back four feet instead of eight. He also agreed to stain the fence to match other community fences and to re-landscape his yard.[2]

Boards should not mindlessly enforce restrictions. They should listen to residents (see the basketball hoop example on page 50). If residents are failing to follow a rule, the problem may be the restriction itself.

Legal Audit

With a legal audit, an attorney reviews all aspects of the association's operations and prepares a report on potential legal risks. An audit ensures that rules and covenants meet federal and state requirements, that they are reasonable and enforceable, and that they aren't outdated. According to Georgia attorney Seth Weissman, who has conducted legal audits for numerous associations, an audit includes these steps:

- Reviewing all association documents, including declarations, by-laws, articles of incorporation, policy resolutions, rules and regulations, minutes, insurance policies, contracts, and correspondence
- Reviewing the association's operations and procedures
- Reviewing dangerous conditions that may exist on the property
- Preparing a report on the areas of legal risk and how these risks can be minimized or eliminated
- Developing and implementing an action plan to minimize legal risks[3]

"Legal counsel should annually review the documents to identify provisions that may be ambiguous, unreasonable, illegal, or otherwise invalid or unenforceable," writes Marvin Nodiff.[4] The attorney may also want the manager's input to determine which rules and restrictions are vague, confusing, or unworkable.

Periodic Reviews

One way to uncover outdated or unenforceable rules is through periodic reviews. Russ Hoselton, PCAM, led such a review at the Kukui Plaza condominium in Honolulu. In 1995, association staff and volunteers reviewed each of the community's rules and regulations. Their mission: to seek out unreasonable and unenforceable rules. "What is the purpose of the rule?" they asked. Is it enforceable? Is it fair? Did it single people out? Is the rule even necessary? Does it address a real problem?

There were 89 rules when they started. Only 32 survived.

According to Hoselton, residents were thrilled by the reduction in rules and voiced their approval at the annual meeting. "The board will spend a lot less time dealing with rule violations and complaints," said Hoselton, in the *Common Ground* article "Bending the Rules." "Living at our community is much easier these days."[5]

Time Limits

A time limit is like setting an alarm clock for your rules. After two years, for example, a rule with a time limit would expire. At that point, the board would examine the rule to ensure it is necessary, legal, and enforceable. If so, the rule would be reinstated for another two years. If not, the rule would be dropped.

Property manager Norman Craig developed a time limit policy for the Holly Hill condominium in Forestville, Maryland. Said Craig: "Staggered expiration dates allow you to review the rule and see if it's still needed. It makes sense. Associations are not stagnant—they are in constant transition. Rule-making needs to take this into consideration."[6]

Amending the Documents

If your association's governing documents are unclear, unreasonable, or out of date, the board may need to amend the documents. Be prepared, however—it can be a difficult task.

Start by contacting your association attorney. The attorney can help the board decide if an amendment is the proper remedy for the problem. As Colorado attorneys Thomas J. Hindman and Lynn S. Jordan note, "Amending CC&Rs to modify behavior—barking dogs, loud stereos—is rarely successful. Behavior problems are better left to rules."[7]

An amendment is probably needed, according to Hindman and Jordan, if the documents:

- Do not comply with state law
- Are ambiguous and difficult to interpret and enforce
- Do not give the association sufficient power to create and successfully enforce the rules
- Do not allow the board to efficiently operate the community or deal with community concerns (such as outdated use restrictions)
- Contain developer "boilerplate" language that is no longer applicable
- Set unreasonable restrictions on the community or do not provide the proper tools for the association to effectively solve specific problems
- Do not have a mechanism to correct previous legal problems

The attorney can also help determine what voting percentages are required—80 percent of the members and 100 percent of the mortgagees is common—and answer the numerous technical questions that will arise. The attorney should draft the amendment as well, to ensure it doesn't conflict with other portions of the documents.

Once the board approves the amendment, it must obtain community support. The best way to do this is by asking members for input early in the process. In addition to learning how members feel, it also allows the board to explain why the amendment is necessary and why—due to high voting percentages—the association needs each member's support.

"Don't forget to listen to your members' comments," write

Hindman and Jordan. "They may be able to point out issues the board had not considered."[8]

Hindman and Jordan also recommend that boards develop a strategy. Documents usually are amended either by a vote held at a meeting or by written consent. If a meeting is required, the board must consider "legal issues, such as notice and quorum requirements, and practical concerns, like the date, time, and location of the meeting.

"If a meeting is not required, the board must decide whether to mail or hand deliver the amendment and consent form, who will do the mailing or canvassing, if signatures must be notarized, if the canvassers are notaries, how much time will elapse before follow-up contacts will be initiated, and how will those contacts be made (by mail, in person, or by telephone)."[9] The association also will need to determine the best way to contact mortgagees, which may include identifying loan numbers and confirming whether the loan has been assigned.

Successful boards then monitor their progress, adjust to changes, track which members (and mortgagees) agree to the amendment, and review returned consents to make sure the signatures are properly notarized (if required) and match the membership roster.

"The board should set realistic goals or benchmarks to measure progress—for example, obtaining 50 percent of the consents one month after mailing them," suggest Hindman and Jordan. "Finishing the project in 90 days is a good target."[10]

If the amendment is approved, it should be recorded or filed where the declaration was recorded. The board may need to take some additional steps depending on the requirements of its governing documents and state statutes. The association's attorney should review these steps and confirm that the board has complied with all legal requirements. "Failure to follow the requirements set out in the governing documents or statutes may serve as grounds for challenging the validity or enforceability of the amendment at a later date."[11] Finally the association should mail the amendment to its members.

CHAPTER FIVE

Conclusion

"Boards must be sensitive to the
balance of power and must not usurp
the rights of their constituents."

—*Massachusetts attorney Seth Emmer*

In late 1996, a Maryland homeowner association
waddled out of a difficult duck dilemma.

The dilemma involved six-year-old Michael Rizzo, a
physically and mentally disabled resident of the West
River Estates community in Annapolis. Rizzo has two pet
ducks, named Daisy and Dipsy. The boy's mother and
neurologist believe the ducks are important to Rizzo's development.

Unfortunately, Daisy and Dipsy began wandering
onto the road—and neighbors began to squawk. In May
1996, the West River Estates association ruled that the
ducks violated a covenant barring the raising of livestock.
Both sides continued to work toward a compromise, however, and in October, the association agreed to make an
exception: it would allow the ducks, provided that they
were confined to a pen. The association also asked the

Rizzos to shield the pen with plantings and to remove a wooden sign stating: "Warning—Ducks Protected by the Vietnam Veterans of America."

The sign was placed by a local chapter of the VVA, which heard Rizzo's story and made him an honorary member. The VVA built the duck's new home—complete with a shingled roof and small pond— and one VVA member, citing Rizzo's courage, gave the boy his purple heart.

It was a happy ending for everyone involved.[1]

Unfortunately, most stories have a different ending. In 1994, Bob Brockett bought a wooden cover for his hot tub. His homeowner association soon informed him that its rules prohibit structures unconnected to the house. Brockett was already in hot water with the Venice Shores association—earlier that year the association had a lien placed on his house when he failed to pay his association assessments. But Brockett protested that the tub cover wasn't a structure. The cover controversy and other resident complaints, as usual, attracted the attention of a local newspaper. The president defended the association's action, and ended his explanation with a simple sentence: "Rules are rules."[2]

The "rules are rules" enforcement philosophy is as old as community associations themselves. For nearly 30 years, since developers formed the first condominium and homeowner associations, boards of directors—and many attorneys—have clung to a sacred yet unwritten belief: thou shalt enforce every rule. Make one exception to the architectural covenants, let one homeowner violate a restriction, and the result will be chaos. Members will rebuild cars on their balconies, they'll fill their yards with garden gnomes and old washing machines, they'll let packs of wild animals roam the streets. Faster than you can put a pink flamingo in your front yard, property values will plummet. Don't enforce a restriction and the board will set a bad precedent.

Brent Herrington, PCAM, believes the words "bad precedent" should be expunged from the vocabulary of community association directors. Herrington, former community manager of Disney's Celebration community in Celebration, Florida, thinks board members are so afraid of setting a bad precedent that they take an unreasonably hard line against members. If a member's new driveway is two inches too wide, boards feel they can't allow it—it will never be able to enforce its driveway guidelines because it set a bad precedent.

"This single phrase, and the irrational fear it engenders, is at the root of more problems than any other in the association universe," said Herrington. "It compels reasonable people to make unreasonable decisions."[3]

It's time for associations to write responsible rules and review existing restrictions. To eliminate restrictions that are outdated and illogical, and to address specific problems with clear, specific solutions. To realize that overzealous, unreasonable boards of directors can be more damaging to property values than the violations they so vigorously try to prevent.

It's time to be reasonable.

NOTES

Introduction

1. Cathy Carroll, "Kiss Kindles Condo Furor," *USA Today*, June 19, 1991. Also see "Condo Apologizes for 'Kiss' Accusation," *USA Today*, June 20, 1991.

Chapter One: Writing Reasonable Rules and Restrictions

1. *M–100: The Essentials of Community Association Management* is an educational course offered nationally as part of CAI's Professional Management Development Program. Massachusetts attorney Stephen Marcus notes that when accommodations and modifications for disabled persons are involved, "the stricter of state or federal law will control."

2. Tina Cassidy, "Every Dog Has His Day," *The Boston Globe*, April 3, 1995.

3. Katharine Rosenberry, *ABCs—A Basic Course for Association Leaders* (Alexandria, VA: Community Associations Institute, 1994), 134.

4. *Hidden Harbor Estates* v. *Norman*, 309 So. 2d 180 (Fla. Dist. Ct. App. 1975). Also see William J. Flynn, "Reasonableness Explained and Defined," *Community Association Law Reporter* (July 1981), 1–3, 7.

5. Ibid.

6. *Nahrstedt* v. *Lakeside Village Condominium Association, Inc.*, Case No. S029132, California Supreme Court, September 2, 1994. Also see "Validity of Pet Restriction Is Determined by Evaluating Development as a Whole," *Community Association Law Reporter* (October 1994), 1–2.

7. "Validity Killed the Cat," *Common Ground* (November/December 1994), 21.

8. Ibid.

9. *Liebler* v. *Point Loma Tennis Club*, 95 Daily Journal D.A.R. 16541 (Cal. App. 1995). Also see "Rule Excluding Nonresident Owners from Use of Facilities Found Reasonable," *Community Association Law Reporter* (June 1996), 5. For a shorter summary see "Ruling Prohibits Nonresident Owner from Using Facilities," *Common Ground* (May/June 1996), 10.

10. *Laguna Royale Owners Association* v. *Darger*, 119 Cal. App. 3d 670, 174 Cal. Rptr. 136 (1981).

11. *Beachwood Villas Condominium* v. *Poor*, 448 So.2d at 1143.

12. Wayne S. Hyatt and Jo Anne P. Stubblefield, "The Identity Crisis of Community Associations: In Search of the Appropriate Analogy," 27 *Real Prop., Prob. & Tr. J.*, 691–692.

13. Ibid.

14. Kenneth Budd, "A Board's Best Friend?," *Common Ground* (March/April 1997), 17.

15. Marvin J. Nodiff, "Decision-Making in the Community Association: Do the Old Rules Still Apply?," *Journal of the Missouri Bar* (May/June 1996), 144.

16. Tom Moroney, "Battle Over a Balcony Barrier," *The Boston Globe*, August 21, 1993.

17. Christine Bertelson, "Why One Boy, 6, Can't Play Outside," *St. Louis Post-Dispatch*, September 12, 1995.

18. *Hawkins* v. *Jamaicaway Place Condominium Trust*, No. 5-5474 Mass. Supreme Judicial Ct., Suffolk Co., April 3, 1991.

19. "Covenants, Security, and Liability," *Common Ground* (November/December 1993), 30.

20. Michele Daly, "Street Fun Gives Way to Safety Concerns," *Acorn* (Aurora, CA), August 23, 1995.

21. *Miesch* v. *Ocean Dunes Homeowners Association, Inc.*, No. 93-CvS-1079, New Hanover County, N.C. App., November 7, 1995. Also see "Neither Governing Documents Nor Statute Authorize Association to Impose User Fees on Renters," *Community Association Law Reporter* (March 1996), 3.

22. *Friedman, et al* v. *Highfield House Condominium, Inc.*, Circuit Court for Baltimore City, Nos. 83290003 and 83279049/E1156 (December 22, 1983).

23. David H. Fishman, "Parking Regulations Struck Down," *Community Association Law Reporter* (June 1984), 1, 8.

24. "Owner Claims Meeting Date Was Religious Discrimination," *Common Ground* (November/December 1997), 12.

25. George E. Nowack, "Full House," *Common Ground* (March/April 1996), 18.

26. Ibid.

27. Seth Emmer, "The Needs of the One" *Common Ground* (March/April 1996), 22.

28. Ibid.

29. Janet L.S. Powers and Timothy Graves, "Dealing with the Disabilities Act," *Common Ground* (January/February 1997), 36. Also see Vickie L. Gaul, "The Americans with Disabilities Act—Navigating Uncharted Waters," *Common Ground* (May/June 1992), 28–32.

30. Rosenberry, *ABCs*, 132.

31. Gurdon H. Buck, *GAP Report #7—Drafting Association Rules* (Alexandria, VA: Community Associations Institute, 1994), 10.

32. "Playing by the Rules," *Common Ground* (July/August 1993), 24.

33. Budd, "A Board's Best Friend?," 16.

34. Kenneth Budd, "Home Is Where the Businesses Are," *Common Ground* (September/October 1991), 27. Also see Thomas C. Schild, "Developing a Policy on Home Businesses," *Common Ground* (January/February 1994), 44.

35. Jay S. Lazega, "Following the Rules Through Friendly Persuasion," *Common Ground* (November/December 1994), 52.

Chapter Two: Reasonable Enforcement Strategies

1. Budd, "A Board's Best Friend?," 20.

2. Denise Palmieri, "Do You Have a Hearing Problem?," *Common Ground* (November/December 1995), 28.

3. "Reactive Enforcement," *Common Ground* (November/December 1997), 16.

4. Ibid.

5. Ibid.

6. Benny L. Kass, "I, Spy," *Common Ground* (November/December 1997), 18.

7. Ibid.

8. "Playing by the Rules," 24.

9. Palmieri, " Hearing Problem?," 28.

10. "Spring Fever, Covenants Blues," *Common Ground* (March/April 1994), 27.

11. F. Scott Jackson and David G. Baratti, *Strategies for Successful Enforcement of Rules and Deed Restrictions* (Alexandria, VA: Community Associations Institute, 1994), 9.

12. Denise Palmieri, "Take Your Time," *Common Ground* (March/April 1996), 29.

13. Both quotes are from the Letters department, *Common Ground* (May/June 1996), 8. The first quote is from Gabriel J. Trepiccione of Bridgewater, New Jersey; the second is from Fred W. Hemric of Hilton Head Island, South Carolina.

14. Pamela Dittmer McKuen, "Ask, Plead, Threaten, Sue," *Chicago Tribune*, July 1, 1994.

15. Palmieri, " Hearing Problem?," 28.

16. Ibid, 26.

17. Ibid, 30–31.

18. David Norvell, "We Can Work It Out," *Common Ground* (September/October 1994), 34.

19. Kenneth Budd, "Give Mediation a Chance," *Common Ground* (January/February 1991), 28.

20. "Go to Your Room!," *Common Ground* (May/June 1995), 25.

21. Andree Brooks, "Finding the Rule Breakers," *New York Times*, September 11, 1994.

22. The tips on pages 35–38 appeared in "Go to Your Room!," 25–26.

23. Kenneth Budd, "Bending the Rules," *Common Ground* (May/June 1995), 19.

24. Ibid.

25. Ibid, 20.

26. "Three Steps for Making Exceptions," *Common Ground* (May/June 1995), 18. This appeared as a sidebar to "Bending the Rules."

27. Ibid.

28. *Riss* v. *Angel*, No. 63898-5, Wash. Supreme Ct., April 10, 1997.

29. "Board is Liable for Damages After Exceeding Architectural Review Authority," *Community Association Law Reporter* (August 1997), 9.

Chapter Three: Restrictions That Cause Controversy

1. Joe Kollin, "Condo Bans Kids from Outside Play," *Sun-Sentinel* (Ft. Lauderdale), July 23, 1995.

2. "Let Condo Children Play: Pact," *Star* (Tinley Park, IL), September 14, 1995.

3. "Families with Children—Do the Kids Have to Stay Inside?," *Common Ground* (March/April 1996), 16. This appeared as a sidebar to "Full House."

4. George E. Nowack, "Don't Enforce Discriminatory Pool Rules," *Common Ground* (March/April 1996), 19. This appeared as a sidebar to "Full House."

5. Nowack, "Full House," 19.

6. "More Flag Disputes in the News," *Common Ground* (September/October 1994), 6.

7. "Playing by the Rules," 26. Also see Alice R. Friedman, "Old Glory Flies," *Common Ground* (July/August 1991), 18–21.

8. "No Season's Greetings Allowed," *Contra Costa Times* (Walnut Creek, CA), December 18, 1996.

9. Diane Brown, "Decorations Divide Condo Complex," *San Gabriel Valley Tribune* (Covina, CA), December 11, 1995.

10. Tim Gerber, "Condo Owner Fined for Holiday Lights," *Chicago Sun-Times*, December 9, 1994.

11. Sallie James, "House from Hell?," *Sun-Sentinel* (Ft. Lauderdale), October 11, 1996.

12. Kenneth Budd, "What's So Scary About Holiday Decorations?," *Common Ground* (September/October 1997), 16–17.

13. "Christmas Covenants." *Common Ground* (November/December 1993), 26.

14. Budd, "Holiday Decorations," 19.

15. Ibid, 17–18. Also see Molly Sinclair, "To Ban on Holiday Lights, He Says, 'Humbug!,'" *The Washington Post*, December 12, 1992, and "Spirit of Season Enlightens Condo Group," December 17, 1992.

16. Ibid, 18.

17. Ibid, 19.

18. John D. Tomlinson, "The Colony Drives Away Popular Violin Teacher," *Californian* (Temucula, CA), July 16, 1996.

19. Jim Kadera, "Not Exactly in Harmony," *Oregonian* (Portland), June 13, 1996.

20. Colleen Bradford, "Piano Lessons in Recess," *St. Louis Post-Dispatch*, May 7, 1996.

21. "Teaching Music, Learning About Covenants," *Common Ground* (January/February 1997), 18.

22. Budd, "Home Is Where the Businesses Are," 25.

23. "Teaching Music, Learning About Covenants," 18.

24. "Georgia Association Engaged in War of the Roses," *Common Ground* (November/December 1995), 6.

25. "Roses Are Red, Owner Is Blue," *Common Ground* (January/February 1994), 8.

26. Roy Wenzl, "Group Seeks to Uproot Homeowner's Tree Garden," *Sun-Sentinel* (Ft. Lauderdale), December 12, 1995.

27. Tom Bayles, "Argument Springs from Condo Garden," *St. Petersburg Times*, January 13, 1996.

28. "Spring Fever," 27.

29. "Hoop Dreams, Rules Nightmare," *Common Ground* (July/August 1996), 10.

30. Kenneth Budd, "Avoiding Hoop Disputes," *Common Ground* (March/April 1998), 34–37. All of the quotes and information on hoops—pages 50–53—first appeared in this article.

31. "Swingsets Are No Fun for Three Associations," *Common Ground* (November/December 1993), 6.

32. Ibid.

33. "Spring Fever," 25–26.

34. Ibid, 26.

35. Steve Rinehart, "Theirs Is a House of a Different Color," *Anchorage Daily News*, September 25, 1993.

36. "With Paint Samples, Owners Aren't Color Blind," *Common Ground* (January/February 1997), 51.

37. Kris J. Sundberg, "The Color Purple," *Common Ground* (November/December 1993), 23.

38. *Board of Directors of 175 East Delaware Place Homeowners Association* v. *Hinojosa*, WL 227343, Ill. App. 1 Dist. (1996). Also see "No-Dog Rule Disallowed," *Community Association Law Reporter* (October 1996), 7.

39. "Illinois Supreme Court May Consider Dog Case," *Common Ground* (September/October 1997), 13. Also see "Homeowner Association May Enforce No-Dog Rule," *Community Association Law Reporter* (July 1997), 6.

40. Budd, "A Board's Best Friend?," 15–20. Most of the quotes and information on pages 56–59 of this book first appeared in this article.

41. CAI has published numerous articles and information on the Telecommunications Act since it was passed into law in 1996. The interpretation of the FCC's antenna rule is based on information from CAI's Government and Public Affairs Department.

42. "A Clearer Picture," *Common Ground* (January/February 1998), 29–34. The case studies and interpretations found on pages 60–61 are based on information from this article.

43. "Adjusting Your Antenna Rules," *Common Ground* (January/February 1997), 40.

44. Ibid.

45. "FCC Still Has Not Issued Common Property Rule," *Common Ground* (January/February 1998), 30. This appeared as a sidebar to "A Clearer Picture."

46. "Book 'Em Danno, Covenant Violation," *Common Ground* (May/June 1992), 7.

47. Mark D. Imbriani, "Election Signs: First Amendment Rights v. Restrictive Covenants," *Common Ground* (May/June 1992), 44. For additional information on this subject, see Katharine Rosenberry, "An Introduction to Constitutional Challenges to Covenant Enforcement," *CAI's Journal of Community Association Law* (Vol. 1, No. 1), 23–31.

48. *Midlake on Big Boulder Lake Condominium Association* v. *Cappuccio*, 449 Pa. Super 124, 673 A.2d 340 (1995). Also see "Enforcement of Covenant Is Not Unconstitutional," *Community Association Law Reporter* (May 1996), 4; "Court Rejects First Amendment Arguments," *Common Ground* (March/April 1996), 10.

49. Paul G. Skalny and Susan R. Rapaport, "Sign of the Times," *Common Ground* (September/October 1994), 30.

50. *City of Ladue* v. *Gilleo* 114 S. Ct. 2038, 129 L.Ed.2d 36 (1994).

51. Jonathan Woolf-Willis, "Getting a Handle on Sign Restrictions," *Common Ground* (September/October 1994), 31.

52. MJ Carscallen, "Car Trouble," *Common Ground* (November/December 1996), 32.

53. Ibid, 28.

54. "Towing All Cars," *Common Ground* (July/August 1994), 7.

55. Carscallen, "Car Trouble," 29.

56. Ibid., 30. *Nuzzo* v. *Board of Managers of Jefferson Village Condominium No. 1*, 1996 WL 366455 (N.Y.A.D. 2 Dept.).

57. Ibid.

58. Hal A. Barrow, "Are Parking Lots Strictly for Cars?," *Common Ground* (September/October 1996), 54.

Chapter Four: Eliminating Unreasonable Rules

1. Marvin J. Nodiff, "Don't Enforce Documents That Violate State Law," *Common Ground* (May/June 1995), 44.

2. Brendan Sobie, "Homeowner, Association Mend Fences After Dispute," *Capital* (Annapolis, MD), October 16, 1996.

3. Seth Weissman, "It's Time for Your Legal Check-Up," *Common Ground* (May/June 1991), 12.

4. Nodiff, "State Law," 44.

5. Budd, "Bending the Rules," 22.

6. Ibid.

7. Thomas J. Hindman and Lynn Jordan, "Amending Your Documents," *Common Ground* (July/August 1995), 28.

8. Ibid, 30.

9. Ibid.

10. Ibid, 31.

11. Ibid.

Chapter Five: Conclusion

1. "Association Compromises in Duck Dilemma," *Common Ground* (January/February 1997), 14.

2. Terry Kosdrosky, "Homeowners Upset with Association," *Macomb Daily* (Mt. Clemens, MI), January 5, 1995.

3. Kenneth Budd, "The Fear of Bad Precedents," *Common Ground* (May/June 1995), 17. This appeared as a sidebar to "Bending the Rules."

INDEX

BIOGRAPHY

Kenneth Budd is former director of publications with the Community Associations Institute and the former editor of *Common Ground*, CAI's award-winning national magazine. Since 1990 he has written over 50 feature articles on condominium and homeowner associations.